T0114129

"Sarah is passionate about all young people being successful in school. Her own educational experience has been working with some of the most challenging and vulnerable young people: this means her practical tips come from her own tried and tested strategies. Sarah always places the child at the heart of all that she does, and inclusion runs through her veins. This book will be a practical and useful resource which will make a real difference to teachers being able to more effectively support all of their learners."

Cath Kitchen, OBE, Chair of the National
Association for Hospital Education

"Supporting children with SEMH (social, emotional and mental health) needs is difficult. It's like juggling a million things on a unicycle. But with the right strategies and tools, we can help them succeed in the classroom and beyond. This book helps classroom teachers choose and use those tools. I appreciate this book because it recognises that their needs are often overlooked. Sarah encourages readers to approach this book with an open mind and a willingness to explore creative solutions to help all children learn, regardless of their challenges."

Abigail Hawkins, FCCT, SENsible SENCO

"A non-judgemental tour of the ways in which young people with SEMH may experience the world, and what we can do to help them at school. As well as a valuable addition to your theoretical knowledge on the topic, you'll also develop the confidence, skills and ideas you need to better support the young people you're working with, right away."

Pooky Knightsmith, Child and Adolescent
Mental Health Expert

ALL ABOUT SEMH

All About SEMH is an accessible and informative guide for secondary school teachers, designed to increase their understanding of social, emotional and mental health needs, and to enhance their toolkit with practical, evidence-informed strategies to support learners in their care.

The book unpicks key terminology and debunks myths and misconceptions, enabling teachers to more easily understand some of the challenges for learners with SEMH needs. It then explores a range of key areas including anxiety, depression, bereavement, obsessive-compulsive disorder and self-harm, and focuses on practical strategies and adaptations that can be made in every classroom. *All About SEMH* includes:

- A comprehensive introduction to social, emotional and mental health needs and the surrounding terms and policies.
- Practical strategies tailored to different conditions to help provide targeted support to secondary school learners.
- Case studies and worked examples to illustrate points in the book, supporting behaviour recognition and developing reader understanding.
- The differences between children's behaviour at home and at school are examined, and the voices of parents of children with SEMH are woven throughout.
- Guidance on safeguarding and when to ask for additional support regarding concerns such as drug abuse or child exploitation.
- Easy to dip in and out of chapters with signposting to further research, resources and support.

This accessible guide is a valuable resource to empower secondary educators, increasing their knowledge and understanding of SEMH, and providing a range of practical strategies to support every learner in their class. It will be essential reading for all secondary school educators, SENCOs and parents who are supporting children with SEMH needs.

Sarah Johnson is the founder of Phoenix Education Consultancy, which helps educational establishments to understand what they are doing well and looks at addressing gaps to improve their service. She previously worked in both primary and secondary mainstream education, including as director of inclusion for a large primary school, and as head of a Secondary Pupil Referral Unit.

ALL ABOUT SEND

Series Advisor: Natalie Packer

All About SEND provides busy teachers and SENCOs with essential guidance and practical strategies to effectively support learner with special educational needs and disabilities. Each accessible and informative book focuses on a common area of need and explores key traits and terminology, debunks myths and misconceptions, and introduces readers to a range of easy-to-implement ideas for practice and concrete solutions to everyday challenges.

ALL ABOUT SEMH

A PRACTICAL GUIDE FOR SECONDARY TEACHERS

Sarah Johnson

Routledge
Taylor & Francis Group

LONDON AND NEW YORK

Designed cover image: © Getty Images

First published 2024
by Routledge
4 Park Square, Milton Park, Abingdon, Oxon OX14 4RN

and by Routledge
605 Third Avenue, New York, NY 10158

Routledge is an imprint of the Taylor & Francis Group, an informa business

© 2024 Sarah Johnson

The right of the author to be identified as author of this work has been
asserted in accordance with sections 77 and 78 of the Copyright, Designs
and Patents Act 1988.

British Library Cataloguing-in-Publication Data
A catalogue record for this book is available from the British Library

ISBN: 978-1-032-22571-5 (hbk)
ISBN: 978-1-032-22568-5 (pbk)
ISBN: 978-1-003-27311-0 (ebk)

DOI: 10.4324/9781003273110

Typeset in Interstate
by Deanta Global Publishing Services, Chennai, India

CONTENTS

FOREWORD

All teachers are teachers of learners with special educational needs and disabilities (SEND). Those professionals who work in truly inclusive schools will understand that SEND is everyone's responsibility. However, the situation has not always been like this. When I started my teaching career 30 years ago, learners who had additional needs were more likely to be seen as the responsibility of the special educational needs coordinator (SENCO). As the person in the school who 'held' the SEND knowledge and expertise, the SENCO would often be a lone force in championing, and meeting, the needs of this particular group of learners.

The picture of education is somewhat different today. The profile of the children and young people we teach continues to change. The impact of the COVID pandemic, for example, has led to an increase in those identified with gaps in their learning or with mental health concerns. The number of learners with complex needs being educated within mainstream schools also continues to rise. As professionals, we now have a greater awareness and understanding of some of the challenges our learners face and, as a result, are more determined to do our best to support them to achieve. We understand that this cannot be the role of one person – the SENCO – alone. Every teacher needs to be a teacher of SEND.

Teaching learners with SEND may be one of the most rewarding things you ever do in your classroom. When you observe a learner who has really struggled to grasp a new idea or concept finally achieve their lightbulb moment, it's all the more sweeter knowing the amount of effort they have put in to get there. However, teaching learners with SEND can also be one of the most challenging aspects of your career. In a 2019 survey[1] carried out by the Department for Education (DfE) in England, the level of confidence amongst teachers in supporting learners with SEND was reported as very low. Relevant professional development in this area is, at best, patchy; only 41% of the teachers surveyed by the DfE felt there was sufficient SEND training in place for all teachers.

So how do we overcome this challenge? Evidence suggests that the best place to start is through the delivery of inclusive, high quality teaching (HQT). As the Education Endowment Foundation (EEF) report[2] tells us, there is no magic bullet for teaching learners with SEND, and to a great extent, good teaching for those with SEND is good teaching for all. This means we need to develop a repertoire of effective teaching strategies such as scaffolding, explicit instruction and use of technology, then use these strategies flexibly to meet the needs of individuals or groups of learners.

Although a focus on effective HQT in the classroom is the starting point, some learners will require more specific teaching methods to meet their individual needs. There is no substitute for really getting to know a child or young person so you can fully understand their personal strengths, potential barriers to learning and what works for them in the classroom. However, it can still be helpful for us as professionals to develop a more general understanding of some of the common areas of need we are likely to come across and to have a range of strategies we can try implementing within our practice. This is where All About SEND can help.

The All About SEND series of books aims to support every teacher to be a teacher of SEND. Each book has been designed to enable teachers and other professionals, such as support staff, to develop their knowledge and understanding of how to effectively promote teaching and learning for those with identified areas of need. The books provide essential information and a range of practical strategies for supporting learners in the classroom. Written by expert practitioners, the guidance has been informed by a wealth of firsthand experience, with the views of children and young people with SEND and their parents taking centre stage.

In this book, *All About SEMH*, author Sarah Johnson provides a fascinating insight into the complexities of some of the social, emotional and mental health needs that an increasing number of our children and young people are facing today. Having worked across a wide range of educational, youth and health settings, Sarah has vast experience in supporting secondary school pupils of all ages by reducing and removing social and emotional barriers to help them access education. As Director of Phoenix Education, she supports practitioners, school leaders, multi-academy trusts and local authorities to ensure every young person can participate in, and enjoy, their education. In *All About SEMH*, Sarah encourages the reader to reflect on their own practice and consider how they may support children with SEMH needs to be included in the classroom and beyond.

Thank you for choosing to read this book and for embracing the challenge of responsibility: every teacher a teacher of SEND.

Natalie Packer
SEND Consultant, Director of NPEC Ltd.
@NataliePacker

NOTES

1 https://assets.publishing.service.gov.uk/government/uploads/system/uploads/attachment_data/file/1063620/SEND_review_right_support_right_place_right_time_accessible.pdf, p. 42.
2 https://educationendowmentfoundation.org.uk/education-evidence/guidance-reports/send.

ACKNOWLEDGEMENTS

I always find writing acknowledgements so difficult. There is often a huge number of people who help with the process of writing – from those who give me emotional support to those who give me the practical support of helping to shape my ideas and thinking. If your name isn't here, it isn't because you've not helped me, but more likely that I've grouped you together with others. For these acknowledgements, I have remained focussed on acknowledging my children as being the cornerstone of the work.

I would like to start with Octavia, who as I type this, is 13 years old. She has been a huge driver in helping me write this book. Not only has she given her time to 'sense check' bits to make sure they are helpful, but also by developing an understanding of the way she sees the world helps me try to make sense for teachers and those who work in education.

Her experience of schooling is very different to my own, but some of the things she tells me help me to consider what is important. I also liked her comment the other day when she said to me, about demonstrating her crochet skills, "I can teach you but you don't have to learn", which made me think about how many children have that experience within the schooling environment and how we translate the act of teaching to the collaborative approach to learning.

My girls Astrid and Iris have been developing and growing; just like the pages of this book have increased, so has their weight and height! Astrid and Iris have been exploring the world around them, and I hope to keep them free of some of the events and difficulties that I talk about here. My strive for them in writing this book is that they feel safe, comfortable and know that they belong in the school environment.

It would be amiss of me to not acknowledge the baby that grows inside me as I am writing this. I began this process not being pregnant and am now two weeks away from meeting my baby girl Zelda. Even though I've not met her, understanding more about how she develops and how I want my family to be continues to teach me daily.

ACRONYMS

ADD	attention deficit disorder
ADHD	attention deficit hyperactivity disorder
ARFID	avoidant/restrictive food intake disorder
CCE	child criminal exploitation
CPD	continuing professional development
CSE	child sexual exploitation
DfE	Department for Education
DSM	*Diagnostic and Statistical Manual of Mental Disorders*
EBSA	emotionally based school avoidance
EHCP	education, health and care plan
EHE	elective home education
GAD	general anxiety disorder
ICD	*International Statistical Classification of Diseases and Related Health Problems*
INSET	in-service training
NHS	National Health Service
OCD	obsessive-compulsive disorder
PE	physical education
PMLD	profound and multiple learning disability
PTSD	post-traumatic stress disorder
SCR	serious case review
SEMH	social, emotional and mental health
SENCO	special educational needs coordinator
SEND	special educational needs and disabilities

Part 1

INTRODUCTION

THE PURPOSE OF THIS BOOK
AND HOW YOU MIGHT USE IT

The purpose of this book is to provide an introductory guide for teachers and support staff to develop strategies to help children that have been identified as having social, emotional and mental health (SEMH) difficulties. This book is specifically aimed at those supporting children who are between the ages of 11 and 18 years old. There is another book as part of this book series that focuses on SEMH and younger children that may also be helpful.

Schools are busy places, so to help you be able to find the information when you need it, the chapters of the book are divided into different diagnoses, profiles or needs. You can choose to either read every page of this book, or you may prefer to use the contents page to read up on specific needs and consider some of the interventions that have been suggested. This book is likely to be helpful for a range of staff in the schooling system: head teachers, special educational needs coordinators (SENCOs), teachers and support staff.

At this stage, I want to reaffirm that I am a teacher and although I have drawn on medical literature such as the *International Statistical Classification of Diseases and Related Health Problems* (ICD), *Diagnostic and Statistical Manual of Mental Disorders* (DSM) and medical journals, I am neither a clinician nor psychologist. I am a teacher and one that feels strongly that children who have social, emotional and mental health needs should be supported to be included, content and safe within the environments in which they learn. I draw heavily upon my previous roles as a teacher in mainstream school, the teacher-in-charge of a psychiatric unit, as well as head of an

DOI: 10.4324/9781003273110-2

alternative provision and local authority provision to support students with medical needs accessing school and providing continuity of service.

The term 'special educational needs and disabilities (SEND)' is an umbrella term which aims to provide a framework for how children might be supported and included in the UK education system. Previous to SEND, other terms used included 'maladjusted' and 'educationally subnormal' (House of Commons, 2006). The Warnock Report (Warnock, 1978) reviewed the educational provision for children having handicaps. The report urges "the merits of a more positive approach, based on the concept of special educational need" (Warnock, 1978). It is further detailed in the report that the term 'maladjusted' is stigmatising and urges the term 'emotional and behavioural disorders' and remarks that we should pay particular attention to the emotional climate, social structure and organisations within a school. Whilst this report is over 40 years old, the consideration of language, the environment a child finds themselves in and organisations of schools are still vitally important reflections for everyone who works in school.

Further to the evolution of the term from maladjusted, to emotional and behavioural difficulties, to the now more frequently used SEMH, we also understand that children are complex. Those children who have SEMH might also have needs not included within this book and not defined as SEMH but certainly affected by it. For example, a child with Prader–Willi syndrome might have mild learning difficulties and increased appetite. They might behave in certain ways in the class to avoid activities they don't like or try to enter the dining room to find food. They might not have been identified as having SEMH as their primary need, but their other needs are likely to have an impact on the SEMH needs.

Despite the aforementioned complexities, this book is an attempt to make things a bit easier for the busy person in the classroom. It is designed for teachers, support staff and other people with a specific interest in this area to be able to pick up a book, reflect on their practice and how they may support children to be included in classroom activities and broader school life. The other books in this series and the knowledge contained therein will likely have significant overlap and helpful information that may influence and inform the reader.

I have worked in education for 20 years in both primary and secondary school environments. This has included being a class teacher in a range of settings. I know only too well the challenge of balancing the needs of over 30 children whilst planning and teaching Citizenship and Personal, Health and Social Education. Or the different and sometimes competing needs of teaching children the primary school curriculum. I have had the joy of being the director of inclusion for a large primary school and provided strategic guidance in supporting children who found being in school and the class difficult. I have also been a form tutor for a large secondary school in London, England, with the associated challenges of teaching and pastoral care in a multi-cultural, inner-city area.

I will start with the premise that teaching children can be incredibly hard. This is in terms of planning, consideration of the different requirements and pressures from the children themselves. Coupled with considering the demands and needs of key stakeholders such as parents/carers, senior leadership teams, the wider community and the range of accountability measures that might be in place, teaching is beyond that which happens in the classroom environment but extends into a range of other facets that require consideration. Some short-hand phrases that you may be aware of and underpin your work include safeguarding, child protection, accessibility and relationships. These all underpin and provide structure to not just our subject knowledge but how children can flourish and feel safe in the classroom environment.

As a teacher or those who regularly support children, you may be acutely aware of these pressures, some of which are competing in nature. Depending on your geographical location and where you have trained, you may espouse infrequent and unstructured training on how to support the children who need your expertise the most.

Whilst training to be a teacher, and this experience is likely to be echoed by others, I felt ill-prepared for the diversity of needs within the classroom environment. Instead, the training offered to me was an afternoon training on SEND (dyslexia in this instance), and it had little or no practical suggestions on how to support children that did not fit in within the narrow scope of the university's definition of SEND.

I was poorly equipped for the classroom environment despite having had a year in the classroom directly working with children during my training. The focus of my training was on subject content, producing lesson plans and curriculum sequencing for most children that I may see in my teaching career; in other words, those children that we may define as 'mainstream' or 'typical' of a class. This meant that I struggled with how to plan effectively for the range of children's needs. Whilst those children with behavioural, learning or attention needs may be seen as 'outliers', as with any career where you meet hundreds and thousands of children, those 'outliers' mount up to a significant number. You are likely to want to ensure that you support all children to learn and flourish in your classroom, not just those who meet a narrow definition of being a 'typical student'. I suspect as you read this you were like me, that you want to make your lessons impart key knowledge, build understanding and captivate children's interests.

My training happened nearly two decades ago. I am hopeful that if you have recently undertaken teacher training that your experiences do not echo mine, and, instead, reading through this book forms a companion to your growing professional body of knowledge. It may even be that this book is on the reading list of your university or another professional body where you are undertaking training. If this is the case, then you are already in a position where you have had more guidance than my own training. I hope this book saves you some time and many mistakes, as well as ignites your curiosity to support all children's needs in the classroom.

Depending on where you are teaching or supporting children, there will be a range of terms that may describe children with difficulties that make it hard to access education due to the way they behave. You may have heard the following phrases in discussions and policy documents:

- social, emotional and mental health needs
- challenging behaviour
- behavioural difficulties
- at risk of exclusion
- emotional behavioural difficulties

You may have heard other terms such as:

- naughty
- poorly behaved
- inattentive
- inappropriate
- violent
- aggressive

In this book, the term 'social, emotional and mental health' is used, as it encapsulates both externalised behaviour (what you might be able to see in the classroom environment and what might be seen as disruptive) and internalised behaviour (how a child feels about being within the classroom and wider school environment).

Within the United Kingdom, SEMH needs are understood to be specific needs characterised by difficulty making and maintaining friendships, attending to and listening to the teacher, and expressing emotions in a way that is manageable in the classroom environment.

Some of these behaviours and challenges may permeate within other parts of the child's life such as at home, and relationships outside of school and within their local community. However, it is important to recognise this is not always the case, and the differing demands and structures of these environments may mean that some things that we see in school are not reported within the other environments and vice versa. Indeed, the case may also be the opposite and you may hear reports from parents/carers about difficult situations that you do not recognise within the school environment. There can be criticism from parents and organisations of disbelief in their experiences in the home environment when a teacher utters the phrase "they are fine at school"'.

As a teacher or other educational professional, you might hear about or see for yourself a range of behaviours such as:

- not listening to a teacher's instructions
- not speaking out loud to an adult or other children and young people
- being distracted and finding it hard to attend to the lesson content
- what appears to be an extreme emotional response to situations (tearfulness, aggression)
- refusal to attend school
- destroying school property
- destruction of own work
- shouting at others
- seeming sad or withdrawn

Meeting the needs of children with SEMH is important; it is important because all children and staff should feel safe and content at school. It is not just about the children who may demonstrate concerning behaviour and what we may define as SEMH needs, but it is also about those children within the school community who may find that their own learning is disrupted by others. The feelings of adults who teach and support those children are also a central concern of this book, as being knowledgeable and feeling empowered with strategies will also support teachers.

Further to this is the idea of the rights of the child. The United Nations Convention on the Rights of the Child enshrines the rights of the child to access an education, and there are no caveats or conditions applied to that. Supporting children by reducing and removing any barriers to education is a way of ensuring children can access education.

Supporting children with SEMH needs is vital in helping them have their needs met within the school environment, reducing exclusions (both suspensions and permanent exclusions) and supporting them in becoming citizens who are economically active and belong to their communities. In addition, meeting children's needs and having a work environment for staff where they feel valued and supported in decision-making is important for staff retention.

Ultimately, the purpose of this book is about supporting those who work with children who may demonstrate some of the aforementioned behaviours. It can be used to 'dip in' in which you can turn to a specific chapter to find out more about specific SEMH needs, in order to consider and utilise practical strategies to implement within the class and within school (for example, moving from one classroom space to another, during playtime or other unstructured times). This book is focussed on older children, their experiences of SEMH and how they may be supported within the classroom and the wider school environment. Some of the topics in this book and strategies may be used with younger children as well, but that is up to the sensitivity of the professional working with the child and having an understanding of their particular needs and developmental stage. Additionally, some key areas such as child criminal exploitation and drug use are not discussed in the context of the SEMH for younger children. This is not to say that these SEMH needs are not an issue for younger children, but they are likely (and hopefully) to be less commonplace. It must be further acknowledged that the children who appear on the SEND register at school (or otherwise identified as having SEND) may be what are often referred to as the tip of the iceberg. Stern recognises that "only [original emphasis] one-third of children with diagnosed emotional disorders actually made it to the special needs register of their school" (2022, p. 163). Some of what is discussed in this book may be unrecognised and unidentified as well as misunderstood.

This book is not meant to serve as a dictate of how things must be done, but one that kindles an interest, enthusiasm and creative exploration in helping children learn, whatever the barriers are to that learning.

From this point onwards you may notice that I utilise the term 'children' along with young people. This is a deliberate decision to reaffirm that those children who are older are still just that, children.

WHAT IS THE INTERNATIONAL AND LOCAL POLICY PICTURE?

The United Nations Convention on the Rights of the Child includes 54 articles, with the latter articles about how governments and adults should work together to protect those rights (UNICEF, n.d.). The reason for me relating SEMH to the Rights of the Child is to reaffirm that supporting children with SEMH is not just a moral imperative but a legal one as well. In the following, I have highlighted articles that are particularly pertinent in understanding the responsibilities of those in supporting those rights and signposting where they link to specific chapters in the book.

- Article 19 (protection from violence, abuse and neglect) – Governments must do all they can to ensure that children are protected from all forms of violence, abuse, neglect and bad treatment by their parents or anyone else who looks after them.

This is particularly relevant to the chapters on child criminal exploitation (CCE; Chapter 10) and criminal sexual exploitation (CSE; Chapter 11) as both include aspects in which children are exploited both sexually and to engage in criminal acts. Further issues relating to trauma, such as the chapters which refer to post-traumatic stress disorder (PTSD; Chapter 19) and emerging personality disorder (Chapter 16), may be particularly relevant.

- Article 28 (right to education) – Every child has the right to an education. Primary education must be free and different forms of secondary education must be available to every

DOI: 10.4324/9781003273110-3

child. Discipline in schools must respect children's dignity and their rights. Richer countries must help poorer countries achieve this.

SEMH is often associated with discussions about discipline and how we might ensure effective discipline whilst also protecting the right of each child in the classroom to learn. This is an underpinning concern of this book. Whilst many of the interventions and strategies come from the position of diagnosis and need, there are some discussions of developing a supporting culture within the school environment.

However, without consideration of developing a positive culture that fosters a sense of belonging and is based on the principles of inclusion, specific interventions for children are unlikely to be particularly effective or sustainable.

- Article 39 (recovery from trauma and reintegration) – Children who have experienced neglect, abuse, exploitation, torture or who are victims of war must receive special support to help them recover their health, dignity, self-respect and social life.

This article most closely links to the section on PTSD but also may be referred to in the context of CCE, CSE and emerging personality disorder.

- Article 40 (juvenile justice) – A child accused or guilty of breaking the law must be treated with dignity and respect. They have the right to legal assistance and a fair trial that takes account of their age. Governments must set a minimum age for children to be tried in a criminal court and manage a justice system that enables children who have been in conflict with the law to reintegrate into society.

Along with the international policy picture stipulated in the articles of children's rights is wider legislation within the UK; this being the Equality Act 2010, for children who may be considered to have a disability, along with the SEND Code of Practice. There are stark warnings that the current local policy picture in the UK leaves children with SEMH vulnerable to exclusion:

> in circumstances of challenges and limited resources, there is heightened risk that pupils with SEMH can become collateral causalities of policy change evacuated to the social margins of schooling.
>
> *(Thompson, Tawell, & Daniels, 2021)*

These tensions often drive dialogue of whether children with SEMH who also interrupt the education of others should be excluded from school and educated elsewhere, and what effective interventions may be needed to include them.

WHAT DOES IT MEAN TO HAVE SOCIAL, EMOTIONAL AND MENTAL HEALTH NEEDS?

Older children with SEMH are at increased risk of exclusion from school, with persistent absences and poorer outcomes. The reasons for this are complex and should not be understood in simplistic terms, but considering the range of intersections between a child's needs, how those needs are met, the schooling environment and the wider social context. When considering what it means to have SEMH needs, we can ask a range of individuals who may be involved in the support of a child, the child themselves and their parents, as well as teachers, social care and other external agencies, where relevant. Following are some examples of parents' and children's experiences of SEMH.

> I often worried about getting things right and that I might upset my teachers if I forgot something that I needed to take to school. At primary school it was kinda okay as there wasn't much to bring. When I went to secondary school it was a bit weird anyway because of COVID, I hadn't really been to school much so getting things sorted was not very easy. I went to secondary school, and was really worried that I would forget something and then I would get a detention and told off. The worry wouldn't go, I would try and pack my bag in the evening like mum said, but sometimes I would still forget. I got some detentions and they weren't bad, you know, they were just a detention, but then I worried that I wouldn't be able to answer a question if a teacher asked me out loud. I started having to count

DOI: 10.4324/9781003273110-4

in my head to a 104, if I didn't get to that number by the time the teacher asked us to do something, it meant that they would ask me something and I wouldn't be able to speak. Like, I know that didn't happen, it never happened. But that was the worry. So eventually, I had more things I had to do in my head before I was able to start work or to answer a question. I would sort of freeze you know? And then I become more and more stuck in the things I had to do in my head and wouldn't be able to respond to the teacher, do the work or much else. I started being quite late for school as all these things I had to do.

(From a 13-year-old with obsessive-compulsive disorder)

My son has generalised anxiety disorder. When he was younger, we thought it was more just refusing to go to school. There would be arguments, refusing to get dressed, put on his shoes and it felt like constantly being defiant. When he was a bit older, he'd get himself to school and that helped, but some days were better than others. He would worry all the time but couldn't tell me what was going on. If anything was going on. He started to not message his friends, playing online, just would sort of hole himself up in the room. In the end, I tried to take him to the GP and he said no for quite a while before I managed to get him there.

(From the parent of a 15-year-old with generalised anxiety disorder)

Florence was never a big fan of school. From primary she used to not like going and I'd have to coax her to attend. Her older brother and sister never an issue, but she would find it hard. The school at primary weren't great, just put her down to being naughty, defiant, whatever phrase. Secondary were even worse as there were higher expectations around her work and what she would be doing. She would walk out of class, argue with teachers. Her sense of fairness was strong as well! If she felt that she had not *been listened to, or that the teacher was not being fair or treated her differently, she would argue. I would see this at home as well, so it wasn't like it was particularly different. Florence would get distracted easily in class, and would much rather be doing something else. At football club she excelled so in the end we decided to pull her out of school. She wasn't getting the help she needed, she was so unhappy and I could see her self-esteem getting worse and worse. She will be going to college next year.*

(From the parent of a 16-year-old with ADHD)

The term SEMH is a broad one, and whilst it is not a diagnosis, the umbrella description may feature a diagnosis as part of an attempt to understand needs. For children in the UK, if you are identified as having SEND there is a growing evidence base that there is an increased chance that you will be permanently excluded or have more absences from school compared to your peers, and this is likely to have an effect on academic outcomes.

PERMANENT EXCLUSION AND SUSPENSIONS

Permanent exclusion in England and Wales describes when a child is expelled from school and it is seen as the most serious sanction that a school can issue for misbehaviour. Only head teachers have the power to permanently exclude a child from school (Gov.uk, 2022b). In England and Wales, head teachers are able to issue an exclusion for behaviour that occurs both in and out of a school. The local authority then has a legal responsibility to organise full-time education for the child after the sixth day from the point of exclusion.

Suspension, sometimes referred to as a fixed-period exclusion, is when a child is temporarily not allowed to attend school. Head teachers can issue suspensions for up to 45 school days in one academic school year. However, the school maintains responsibility for the child in that it must set and mark work for the first five school days and arrange suitable full-time education from the sixth (Gov.uk, 2022b). These alternative arrangements may be in Pupil Referral Units (PRUs), Alternative Provisions (APs), or more unusually home tuition or virtual learning platforms.

Much concern has been expressed in England and Wales about the issuance of exclusions and suspensions. Concerns are raised about the overrepresentation of children:

- from specific ethnic groups
- with specific deprivation indexes (for example, free school meals)
- with SEND
- with social care involvement

Whilst these are important considerations, and especially relevant to thinking about intersectionality, I will not be focussing on these broad themes, as this is not the remit of this book. Instead, I will focus on SEMH and exclusions, and draw your attention to other relevant literature (Stern, 2022; Timpson, 2019).

In Stern's (2022) work on permanent exclusion and suspensions there is a detailed analysis of the interplay between SEND and the impact it has on children. The research is focussed on the UK, and those reading this book beyond the UK will likely have different data they can refer to. Regardless of location, those who are reading this book will probably find that Stern's work resonates with their own specific context. Stern acknowledges that within England, children who are identified as having SEN are five times more likely to be excluded from school compared to those without such identified needs.

ABSENCES FROM SCHOOL

In UK policy and lobbying there have been strong demands for schools to improve attendance. Some of the concerns cited about lack of attendance include safeguarding as well as poorer academic outcomes. In contrast, some parents and organisations as well as school leaders argue that school attendance is not an effective proxy of progress or attainment. Moreover, poorer attendance may be a symptom of a child struggling in the schooling environment. It is worth noting that there is little data in the UK on how many children with medical needs (which can be as varied as recovery from operation, chronic conditions such as cystic fibrosis, or significant mental health needs such as psychosis or clinical depression) are persistently absent from school. Instead, the data is collected in larger data sets which do not capture specific reasons for absence, making it difficult to explore the nature of the medical need that is preventing attendance to school.

In the UK there are specific requirements and legislation concerning a child being provided with a suitable education. Whereas in some other European countries (such as Germany) you must send a child to school, in the UK, you can decide to educate your child without sending them to school (for example, within the home). This is frequently referred to as elective home education.

However, most children in the UK between the ages of 4 and 16 are on roll in a school and attend school regularly. Nonetheless, there are still children who are persistently absent from school. Persistence absence refers to children who are absent from school for more than 10% of available opportunities in which to attend.

In the autumn term of 2021/22, the Department for Educations (DfE) presented data which indicated that a child is more likely to be absent from school if they attend a special school compared to mainstream primary or secondary school (Gov.uk, 2022a). The data must also be understood in the context of the COVID-19 pandemic as well as illnesses such as coughs, colds etc., preventing children from attending school. Additionally, children with SEND in mainstream schools are more likely to be absent compared to their peers who do not have identified SEND.

Children in special schools may include those with profound and multiple learning disabilities (PMLD) and have more health needs, increasing a propensity for absences from school. Other children may be absent because of SEMH needs preventing school attendance (for example, anxiety or mood disorders).

The latter is the focus of this book, with reviewing of strategies that may help children be able to not only attend school but also be able to enjoy it and communicate with others about what may be difficult for them.

Comparing data of children with identified SEMH needs to their mainstream peers demonstrates a wide differential between absence rates. In 2020/21, the DfE recorded the following absence rates:

- SEND with primary need recorded as SEMH, 10.6%
- No identified SEND, 3.9%

(Gov.uk, 2023)

There are suppositions which suggest that 522,000 children in the UK are persistently absent from school due to health needs (No Isolation, 2021). In summary, those children with SEMH needs have higher rates of persistent absences compared to those children without SEMH (Thompson, Tawell, & Daniels, 2021).

ACADEMIC OUTCOMES

The question of whether a child with SEMH needs should be seen as having special educational needs is an important one. There is significant evidence that children that have SEMH needs are less likely to achieve academic outcomes comparable to their peers, or have successful outcomes relating to further education, employment and training (Thompson, Tawell, & Daniels, 2021). This makes the answer of whether there should be specific time, training and resource allocation to children with SEMH needs a resounding yes.

There are several considerations when thinking about the link between SEMH needs and academic outcomes. If children are finding it difficult to process information, concentrate, listen, and attend or even leave the house, it can have fundamental implications on their ability to learn. Whilst some children may be able to self-direct their learning, many will likely struggle to be able to take formal examinations and learn about more complex subjects.

There have been several studies which reviewed the academic outcomes of a child that has been identified as having SEMH needs, and we might also want to include in this mix those children who attend PRUs and APs who may have unidentified SEND. PRUs and APs are educational provisions for children who have been excluded from school, are at risk of exclusion from school or have medical needs that make it difficult to attend their mainstream school.

The Timpson review indicated that in analysing 2015/16 data, 7% of children who were permanently excluded and 18% of children who had repeated suspensions achieved what was deemed as good passes in maths and English for the General Certificate in Secondary Education (GCSE) (Timpson, 2019). This in turn can have an impact on future options with certain qualification routes not being open to those children for further education.

4

DISCUSSING AND FINDING OUT ABOUT RESEARCH ON SEMH

In the UK there have been several recent commissioned reports, research and consideration around SEMH (Stern, 2022; Timpson, 2019; Thompson, Tawell, & Daniels, 2021). I have drawn upon this research to develop a wider understanding of SEMH and specific areas of concern. I strongly recommend that if a piece of research you are reading refers to a primary source of research, read that article or research. Your interpretation or understanding may be different to that of the author who references it. This critical thinking around what is presented is very important, and whilst I have referred to research and policy documents, this is with my own lens of understanding.

Whilst this may seem at odds to include in a book aimed towards educational practitioners, there is so much information out there with varying levels of credibility and expertise that underpins it. To help you find out more about specific areas and apply critical knowledge, I advise the following:

- Look up primary sources to develop your own understanding.
- When was the document published?
- Is there more information that critiques or adds to the body of research?
- Who commissioned and funded the research, and for what purpose?
- Does the research draw upon ethical guidance such as the British Psychological Society or British Educational Research Association? If not, why not?
- What are the credentials of the person/organisation who has presented the data?

DOI: 10.4324/9781003273110-5

Another note to consider is the use of language and case studies within this book. Many of the topics discussed are emotionally challenging; they explore situations where children are in distress and show their distress in difficult ways. Some conversations may resonate with the reader or, if you decide to use the material for wider training or staffing discussions, those individuals who attend. The chapters relating to child criminal exploitation (Chapter 10) and child sexual exploitation (Chapter 11) may be especially distressing to read. As you read this book, looking after yourself as well as the students you work with is incredibly important, and I would stress the importance of activities such as supervision with managers or other employment assistant programmes.

5

SECONDARY SCHOOL

In the UK education system, children often move from primary to secondary school. Primary school in the UK is most frequently one setting from the ages of 4 to 11 before moving to secondary school, which remains compulsory education from the ages of 11 to 16. Children between the ages of 16 and 18 may choose to undertake an apprenticeship within the workplace, but many will continue their studies at college or sixth form in schools where they often decrease the subjects they study and specialise accordingly. Depending on the country's education system in which you work, the children that you teach and support are likely to change from one school to another at a certain age, which may have specific challenges relating to that transition. For example, in the UK it is typical to start primary school the September after a child's fourth birthday, before changing to secondary school at 11 years of age. Alongside the physical location of the school likely changing, so too do routines, expectations and rules. Also, children's friendship groups and relationships with teachers will likely be subject to change. All of this can influence a child's social, emotional and mental health. Their needs may be expressed through their behaviour, concentration, variability in friendships and how they might follow instructions from teachers.

In secondary school, there is likely to be increasing demands and expectations on the young person which may differ from that when they were younger. For example, we might anticipate that a 6-year-old might find it hard to listen and attend for long amounts of time, whilst being less tolerant of a 15-year-old exhibiting the same behaviour. We are likely to also expect a 14-year-old to have better concentration, be less distractable and be better organised. However, some children might find this

DOI: 10.4324/9781003273110-6

challenging as they age for lots of different reasons, some of which are explained in the following pages of this book.

The SEMH needs explored in this book are focussed on older children and how their needs might manifest considering their ages and their own specific context. To this end, a child with the same diagnosis of anxiety may present very differently when they are 5 years old compared to their 14-year-old future self with the same diagnosis.

There is another book in this series which focusses on the needs of primary school children: *All About SEMH: A Practical Guide for Primary Teachers*. If you have read that book as well, you may notice that some of the difficulties discussed in this secondary book do not feature within the primary version. For example, criminal exploitation only features in this book with the view that whilst sadly there are still examples of younger children being involved in criminal and sexual exploitation, there are fewer examples, and the need is more likely to be sup-ported beyond the realms of the school. However, the version for younger children may still be helpful in that it more deeply explores issues concerning attachment and child development, which are omitted from this book but are considered broadly in terms of risk factors related to child sexual exploitation and child criminal exploitation.

This book presents a delineation of SEMH relating to age and interventions; however, I would emphasise that childhood, ado-lescence and, in turn, adulthood are complex processes that do not follow neat packages of chronological steps.

In Part 2, there is an exploration of the different needs that children may have that relate to SEMH, beginning with anxiety and finishing with psychosis and set out in alphabetical order. In each chapter, you will find out a bit about the need or diagnosis. The purpose of this is to help those who work in education have an overview of how these conditions may be diagnosed, what might be some of the things you notice and how it might impact a child directly within the schooling setting. Also provided are a number of tools and interventions that are likely to be helpful to support a child directly in either the classroom or the wider schooling community.

Part 2

DIFFERENT NEEDS AND PRACTICAL STRATEGIES

ANXIETY

Anxiety is the feeling of worry or fear that may be present in some-one's life. Anxiety is highly relevant to a book aimed at those who work with children, as it is the most common psychiatric condition in young people. However, the additional challenge is that the majority of children with anxiety are unlikely to access clinical services (Creswell, Waite, & Cooper, 2014). Please note that whilst obsessive-compulsive disorder (OCD) fits within the remit of anxiety, it is presented in a different chapter (see Chapter 18), as it may require specific support and interventions that are less likely to be helpful within the context of overall support for anxiety.

It is entirely possible that anyone reading this book has also had similar feelings of anxiety at some point in their lives. For many people, these are fleeting feelings, whilst for others they might be more significant and affect their daily lives. These feelings of worry may be felt prior to a test, a presentation in front of others, or when starting a new school or job. Anxiety may be considered an SEMH need if it affects a child's life and their ability to engage in everyday activities.

Anxiety may be felt physically, and you might have heard the following descriptions that could suggest a child is worried in the absence of any specific physical need:

- I feel sick to my stomach.
- I have butterflies in my tummy.
- I'm going to be sick.
- I can't breathe.

Our feelings are felt in the body, and this includes feeling worried about something (Zandt & Barrett, 2021). Children might feel that their hearts are beating fast, that they feel shaky, have

DOI: 10.4324/9781003273110-8

a headache, or may feel sweaty and clammy. Children notic-
ing what is happening in their bodies is an important way of
them developing strategies to help them with anxiety (Zandt &
Barrett, 2021, p. 75).

Other children may demonstrate their anxiety through
somatic symptoms. Somatic refers to the physical manifesta-
tion of emotions; this might be headaches, tiredness, chest
pains, or the need to urinate or defecate. More unusually, some
children might express pain in their joints or not be able to walk.

When thinking about a school-based approach to support
children with anxiety there are different strategies that can
be developed and considered. For example, imagine a triangle,
where the base represents the majority of the children until it
reaches its peak of fewer children who might require more significant support.

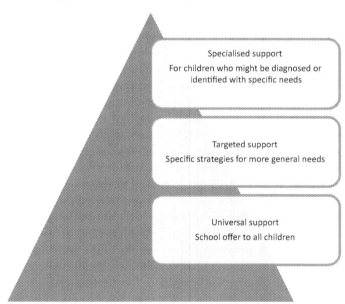

First is the universal support; this is what you as a school would
offer all children, and for the most part that will be enough.
This support might include considering the environment and

communicating changes in routines and curriculum arrangements which promote emotional well-being. Next is targeted support, which includes specific strategies to reduce anxiety such as the use of now and next cards so children know what to expect from one moment to another, or perhaps the use of a toilet pass if they find they worry about not being allowed to use the toilet. Last is the use of more specialised support for children who may be diagnosed with an anxiety disorder, or who are having more specific difficulties within the classroom and schooling environment.

Throughout, the key to any suggestions, tools or interventions is having close dialogue and discussion with parents/carers as well as the young person themselves. This will help in making sure that all are promoting the well-being of the young person. There are effective ways of supporting a child to feel less anxious across all environments that may have specific and different challenges.

The following sections look at more specific issues/difficulties or diagnoses which may be related to anxiety. I explain what some of these difficulties are, how they may present in the school environment and strategies that may be supportive in minimising some of these challenges.

EMOTIONALLY BASED SCHOOL AVOIDANCE (EBSA)

Emotionally based school avoidance (EBSA) is not a medical diagnosis, but a term which reflects growing concerns of persistent absence from school. You may have heard EBSA being referred to in different ways, and with different connotations associated with those terms such as school refusal, absenteeism, non-attendance or even truancy for when we do not know the reasons for a child's absence from school. For example, using the term 'refusal' alludes to the idea that children are being obstinate and defiant in attending school, and therefore the solution to this is geared towards consequences and punishment. On the other hand, EBSA acknowledges that a child may be struggling with the emotional aspect of attending school, and needs intervention, strategies and support to be able to manage those difficult feelings.

Persistent absence from school is certainly not a new phenomenon and was discussed as early as 1932 with Broadwin describing 'truancy' as requiring a need to understand the child as a whole, stating that we should move beyond dictionary definitions but instead strive to understand the child by

> the study of his unconscious psychic life, by the study of his instinctual strivings, their evolution and forms of expression. These unconscious or instinctual forces underlying behaviour follow a pattern which represents the type of adjustment the child has made to his environment, his parents, his siblings, and substitute parents and substitute siblings.

In considering Broadwin's statement and the body of evidence relating to EBSA, two distinct factors are important to consider. One being inherent in the term, that there are emotional factors, and the other being that these emotional factors lead to a lack of attendance at school. EBSA may not just be caused by anxiety (perhaps a worry about attending school, concerns about sensory difficulties or specific anxieties within the school itself) but also because of depression (lack of interest in activities, motivation or seeing friends). There may be other difficulties with the school environment such as those within the environmental and sensory needs. For others, it may involve the challenges of developing and sustaining relationships with peers or conflict with adults in the environments. It is most likely a mixture of different factors that will affect a child's attendance to school rather than one specific cause, and whilst I have included this section within the context of anxiety, please review other chapters (or resources beyond this book) that may also support developing a deeper understanding of this important issue.

GENERALISED ANXIETY DISORDER (GAD)

The most common anxiety disorder, generalised anxiety disorder (GAD) is excessive worry about everyday things that we might not be able to control. These worries will be expressed on most days and for at least six months (Gale & Millichamp, 2016). Symptoms of GAD include:

- feelings of being 'restless' or on edge
- becoming tired easily
- finding it hard to concentrate
- experiences of 'mind going blank'
- being irritable
- finding it hard to get to sleep, or staying asleep or waking up feeling unrefreshed
- feelings of tension in muscles

(American Psychiatric Association, 2013)

Children with GAD are likely to have many overlaps with other anxiety disorders, with 14% of children with GAD also having comorbidity with other anxiety disorders (Gale & Millichamp, 2016). Comorbidity is a term which refers to more than one condition being present at the same time. For example, a child with GAD may also have OCD. GAD can be debilitating, as adolescents may not be able to identify a particular cause of their worry but instead have overwhelming feelings of dread that isolate them from their peers and other activities they might otherwise enjoy. However, worries about performance in schools and family matters feature more so within the other anxiety disorders. It is therefore likely that if you have a child in your class or school with a diagnosis of GAD, compared to, say, a phobia, then you are likely to see aspects of anxiety within the classroom, completion of homework or attending school in the first place.

SOCIAL ANXIETY DISORDER

You may have heard the term 'social anxiety disorder' being referred to as 'social phobia'. Social anxiety disorder in children and adolescents includes the following symptoms:

- Anxiety about at least one social situation in which you might be scrutinised by others. For example, having a conversation, being in class, someone seeing you eat or drink, or performing in front of others. This worry has to be with a child's peers and not just an adult.

- Social situations must nearly always present fear or worry.
- That fear or worry must be disproportionate to the situation.
- These situations are either avoided or if unavoidable experienced with intense feelings of worry and anxiety.
- These feelings last for six months or longer.

(American Psychiatric Association, 2013)

The education system, and particularly schools, feature many social situations in which there are elongated periods of time with others. EBSA in particular may be a feature of social anxiety disorder in considering the criteria of situations (in this case school) being avoided.

INTERVENTIONS AND STRATEGIES FOR CHILDREN WITH ANXIETY DISORDERS

⚙ ANXIETY DISORDER TOOL 1: EXPLICITLY TEACH WORRIES, ANXIETY AND RESPONSES TO THREAT

A key aspect of supporting children with anxiety is enabling them to understand how we respond to threats or perceived threats. Some children may require explicit teaching of this, as they may not be able to pick up on their physical responses and understand. One approach I use is by referencing different examples and discussing how we might typically respond to threats and how anxiety is the physical response without necessarily the threat.

For example, consider the following images of a person responding to a bee. The thing which the person is responding to is the same, but how the person responds depends on their own contexts. A parent may have shown an interest in a bee and looked to provide it with sugar water to help it continue its journey, as in the first picture. Or perhaps the person has been stung before or a parent has demonstrated a fear of that creature, as in the second picture. Our responses to perceived threats or even in the absence of threats can be dependent on a range of factors: our experiences, our cultural references, how others around us may respond.

Figure 6.1 Saving a bee.

Figure 6.2 Running away from a bee.

Responding to threats is often referred to in the following shorthand:

Type of response	What does it mean?	How might you feel?
Flight	To run away or evade the threat	You might feel that you need to get up, that you are trapped and feel tense. You might feel that you are tapping your feet, or feel restless or fidgety. Others might notice that you are red in the face and have dilated pupils.
Fight	To face the danger directly with aggression	You might have a grinding or tight feeling in your jaw, with the urge to punch something or even someone. You might feel very angry. Some people might cry because they feel angry. You might have a feeling of knots in your tummy. You might respond physically to the source of the perceived threat or danger.
Freeze	You are unable to move away or deal with the threat	You might find that your heart rate slows down, you can't move from the spot, or you feel stiff or heavy. You might hear your loud pounding heart rate. There is a sense of dread. Others might say that you have pale skin.

Understanding how different animals, including humans, present anxiety as a stress response can also be an interesting approach to understanding the diversity of responses to threats. Next, I include some case studies of different animals that you can use for discussion purposes. Each case study explores different responses to a threat. A reminder: anxiety is beyond that of a typical response to stress, and whilst may have begun as a protective factor; for some, the physiological response is more intense and troublesome for daily living.

ANXIETY ANIMAL CASE STUDY 1: HONEY BADGER – FIGHT

Honey badgers live across the continent of Africa and can grow as long as 30 inches and be as tall as 11 inches. Despite their size, they have a reputation for being aggressive to predators larger than them (such as lions or hyenas). Honey badgers are reported to protect their homes from large animals such as rhinoceroses. Honey badgers will also fight more than one lion at a time.

Figure 6.3 Fight: honey badger.

ANXIETY ANIMAL CASE STUDY 2:
ELEPHANT SHREW – FLIGHT

Elephant shrews are about the size of a mouse, and yet they can jump about three feet into the air. They can run as fast as 18 miles per hour, which is probably very helpful considering they have many predators, such as snakes, birds and large mammals.

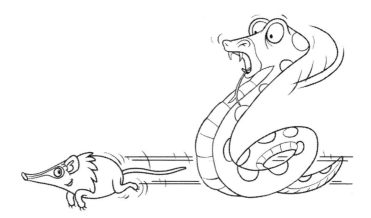

Figure 6.4 Flight: elephant shrew.

ANXIETY ANIMAL CASE STUDY 3:
FAINTING GOATS – FREEZE

Another name for the fainting goat is the myotonic goat, which has a specific condition that means it stiffens and falls over when it becomes excited or startled by something in its environment. This means that if there is a loud noise, a threat or something unexpected in their environment, they are likely to 'faint' and fall over.

Figure 6.5 Freeze: fainting goats.

After reading and discussing the preceding case studies, ask the young person to write their own brief case study about humans and how they are designed to respond to threats from others. Do they see any of the behaviours within their own case study? Or are there bits they would add or amend to make it a personal case study?

 ANXIETY DISORDER TOOL 2: HELP ADOLESCENTS RECOGNISE THEIR COPING STRATEGIES AND ENSURE THEIR AVAILABILITY

Helping adolescents recognise their own individual coping strategies is an important way to support them in being able to manage within the school environment. Everyone will have different coping strategies and it might be that you have to present a range and explore with the child individually. For others, it might be they already know what might be helpful but need to ensure that it is accessible within the school environment. For example, some might know that when they feel anxious, they feel like they need to use the toilet, or even just knowing that they have free access to leave the classroom when necessary can make all the difference to those feelings of worry. In those instances, the use of a toilet pass might be all that is needed for the child to feel empowered to leave the classroom, without even using the pass. For others, it might be specific breathing exercises, fidget toys or a quiet space that helps. If the young person has individual counselling or therapeutic input, it might be that you are able to liaise with them and the young person directly to find out more about what their coping strategies are. The key aspect for the school environment is to ensure the availability of the coping strategy and that those relevant staff are also made aware so that the young person is not denied the opportunity to access or use the coping strategy when relevant.

ANXIETY DISORDER TOOL 3: NOTICE CHANGES AND RESPOND TO THEM

Anxiety is not a fixed state of being. There will be times in which a young person is more anxious than others, but it may not be the case that these are obvious to either the individual affected by anxiety or by those around them. It might be that there are subtle clues, such as a child's lateness to school, preferring to spend time on their own during lunchtime rather than be with others or avoidance of subjects that cause more anxiety than others (for example, physical education or lessons which demand more student discussion). The sharing of this information between teachers may be helpful to recognize that there are mood changes. Other children may be able to identify their variable mood relating to anxiety and be able to symbolise it with you through different strategies, such as the use of different coloured bands on their wrist, e.g. red for anxious and require leaving the room, amber for someone to approach the child and support, green for well and do not need support.

SUMMARY

- Anxiety disorder is an umbrella term which includes other, more specific diagnoses.
- Normal feelings of worry are different to that of an anxiety disorder.
- Anxiety disorders are the most frequently diagnosed mental health disorder for adolescents.
- To help develop coping strategies, it is helpful for children to understand where stress responses come from as well as understand how anxiety manifests in their behaviour.

7

ATTENTION DEFICIT HYPERACTIVITY DISORDER (ADHD) AND ATTENTION DEFICIT DISORDER (ADD)

Attention deficit hyperactivity disorder (ADHD) is diagnosed based on the presentation of several behaviours relating to inattentiveness, hyperactivity and impulsiveness. Whilst a person's symptoms must be present before 12 years of age and for at least six months, it would not be unusual for a teenager or even an adult to be diagnosed at a later age. To address questions of different boundaries or responses to social interactions, symptoms must also be present in two different settings (for example, home and school) (NHS, 2021). There are numerous conversations in literature around whether ADHD should be considered a disorder from a medical perspective or that ADHD is part of neurodiversity. Further, the term 'disorder' does not capture a child's individual strengths which may help within a range of settings (Honos-Webb, 2010; Hartmann, 2015).

ADHD and attention deficit disorder (ADD) were first discussed in the second edition *Diagnostic and Statistical Manual of Mental Disorders* in 1968 (American Psychiatric Association, 1968). ADHD has had several different names which highlight some of the key difficulties that children diagnosed may experience. It was formally referred to as 'hyperkinetic reaction of childhood' before being characterised as a mental disorder in the 1960s, before the more familiar 'attention deficit disorder with or without hyperactivity'.

ADHD is classified under the umbrella of neurodevelopmental disorders, being a condition which emanates from the development of the brain and how it functions. An adolescent with ADHD would need to have symptoms, as described next, before

DOI: 10.4324/9781003273110-9

the age of 12. Unfortunately, for some, the challenges with understanding the nature of an individual's needs and accessing clinical services can make it difficult to achieve a diagnosis at a young age. This does not signify that a child diagnosed at an older age has fewer difficulties with symptoms.

Inattentiveness	
Having a short attention span	Missed instructions from teachers, not being able to follow the class routines
Easily distractable	Being aware of what is happening outside of the classroom and not being able to focus on work
Forgetfulness	Not bringing items into school such as pens or homework, or forgetting to remind parents/carers of school-based events
Losing things	Misplacing PE kit, pens, pencil cases, homework etc
Not completing tasks	Not finishing schoolwork during designated time, handing work in that is unfinished, late to hand in tasks
Difficulty with organising tasks	Late to hand in tasks, difficulty starting tasks, not reading the instructions on set activities
Not completing tasks	Not finishing their schoolwork during designated time, handing in work that is unfinished, late to hand in tasks

Hyperactivity and impulsiveness	
Finding it difficult to sit still	Needing to get up and move around Requirement to fidget, doodle or do something else
Being unable to concentrate on tasks	Losing attention and doing something else
Lots of talking	Talking to those around them, turning around in their seats, speaking out loud

(Continued)

Finding it difficult to wait their turn in conversations or activities	Wanting to say things quickly and seemingly out of the normal flow of conversation
Act without necessarily thinking through consequences	Engage in more mischievous behaviour, not thinking about how their actions may then affect others
Limited sense of risk and danger	Not following through with school rules that are meant to minimise risk, such as wearing safety equipment for science or following instructions about specific routes to take around school

Some of the challenges with ADHD in older children are particularly evident when a child's special educational needs are not recognised and instead a child is labelled as 'naughty' or 'disruptive'. In the UK, a child can be excluded under the category of persistent disruptive behaviour, and it is easy to see how the aforementioned behaviours may fall into this category without necessarily understanding the root cause of what may be underpinning the behaviours. Further complicating this is that children with other needs such as the ill-effects of trauma or foetal alcohol syndrome disorder (FASD) may exhibit behaviours that present as ADHD but require different approaches or sensitivity around this.

INTERVENTIONS AND STRATEGIES FOR ADHD AND ADD

ADHD/ADD TOOL 1: ACADEMIC MENTORING

Academic mentoring refers to a specific mentoring approach which appreciates the particular challenges that a young person may have regarding their ADHD and addresses some of those difficulties. This mentoring approach does not assume a one size fits all. Children with ADHD may have differing levels of inattention, hyperactivity and so on. The mentee (the young person) is partnered with an adult to look at where the mentee's areas of strengths and difficulties are and look at approaches to ameliorate some of those challenges experienced.

A particular programme evaluated within the US is the Challenging Horizons Programme. In this programme, students meet with staff several times during the school week, focussing on organisation skills and how students might approach studying/revising for key subject areas. There are a significant number of opportunities for the student to be able to practise skills as well as be provided with feedback on how they are doing (Evans, Schultz, DeMars, & Davis, 2011). This circular approach, of planning, intervention and rechecking, has been shown to benefit children academically.

ADHD/ADD TOOL 2: VARY TEACHER INSTRUCTION

With older students, we might be used to providing instructions with more than one step that requires following. However, children with ADHD may find it hard to follow such instructions. Instead, the use of one-step instructions can be a helpful way to ensure that all children are on the same stage of instruction. Incorporating the use of one-step instructions within your class need not be arduous and may be something that you reaffirm in a class presentation or workbook. For example, consider the following instructions: "Go to page 16 where you can find the quotes of Macbeth introduced. Using that information find out where Macbeth is described as being heroic and strong. What literary techniques are being used?' You can see with this example that there might be only certain aspects which are picked up by a student who might be distracted or inattentive. Instead, delivering instructions step by step is likely to be more beneficial for children with ADHD. However, it is noteworthy that whilst this might benefit some children, it might frustrate others. If this is the case, you can provide a summary on the board or on a specific resource for the young people that require it. Some examples of one-step instructions are given next to help you think of the language of teacher instruction that you may use in the classroom. It is also helpful to direct the instruction to the individual child so that they know you are speaking to them and it is not general instruction to the whole class.

Anjay, open the book, please.	Name first
	Instruction next
	Modifier for politeness
Olivia, can you check that you have capital letters in your writing, thank you?	Name first
	Instruction to check work
	Modifier for politeness
Amy, sit down first, thank you.	Name first
	Clear instruction before start of lesson
	Modifier for politeness
Daniel, I like how you have answered the question on why the world war started. Well done!	Name first
	Ensure you provide praise for students and not just instructions

Whilst giving teaching instruction, it is important to make sure that you modify your voice and tone to ensure that your student keeps their interest in the instruction itself. It also marks to the person that there has been a change of pace and to redirect attention if they are otherwise distracted.

ADHD/ADD TOOL 3: SUPPORTIVE CHECKS AND REMINDERS

Whilst we may expect most young people to be able to organise themselves with equipment, it can be challenging for those with ADHD. Add to the mix that some of the adolescents that you teach may go back and forth between two parental households or have timetables that change frequently, making organisation even more difficult. Rather than adopting a punitive approach for forgetting items or misplacing them, build in a system of supportive checks for the young person so that you become their champion. This does not have to be something that is intrusive but a quick and simple "just checking you have your calculator with you today as we are doing some work on algebra", or reaffirming any changes in the school timetable by reminding verbally and prompting by pointing to a visual poster, "Just to remind you that tomorrow you will need your sports kit as we have an off-timetable day".

It is also helpful to have spare classroom resources so that if a child has forgotten school equipment (e.g. pen, pencil) that there are some available for them to use.

Also, colour code and/or use symbols in the school timetable; ensure students have several copies and that spare copies are available at a specific location.

ADHD/ADD TOOL 4: CLASSROOM SEATING PLANS

Deciding where children sit in the classroom is full of challenges. Making decisions about how your desks and chairs are set up and then where children may sit is not an easy task. You may also have specific requirements detailed by the school leadership team about how a classroom should be set up, in addition to the practicalities of moving from class to class and having the time to move around classroom equipment.

However, some tips that may be more realistic are to consider the distractions and the environment around the child, For example, is there air-conditioning that hums or a light that flickers that may be particularly distracting for someone with ADHD? Perhaps, there is a window that has frequent movement outside, which could be another additional distraction.

Another consideration is the position of a student in relation to the teacher. It is likely that you move around the classroom, but there might be specific areas in the classroom where it might be more difficult to see a child. I would therefore recommend avoiding these places for children generally, but especially those children with ADHD when you might want to target additional support.

Finally, when thinking about classroom seating plans, consider that a child may require additional movement breaks or the ability to leave the classroom unimpeded. For example, a classroom needs to have a clear pathway to exit with the use of a time-out card. Or consider the approach of allowing 'movement breaks' where a child is allowed to get out of their seat to do a positive activity. You may ask the child to get their book or some other equipment. It is helpful to ensure that the movement break is meaningful and has a physical distance from the seat to wherever the books/equipment or so on are kept so it is more than just a tokenistic gesture.

SUMMARY

- ADHD is the most common neurodevelopmental disorder.
- ADHD can make it hard for a child to sit still and concentrate within the classroom setting.
- Children with ADHD may demonstrate impulsive behaviour.

8

BEREAVEMENT, GRIEF AND LOSS

Bereavement and loss are part of the human experience, but that doesn't make it any easier to deal with. You are likely to have had your own experience of bereavement and loss, whether that be the death of a loved one or perhaps a loss in terms of marriage separation or the dislocation felt when you have moved from one country to another.

The term 'grief' refers to the emotional response when someone dies. The ways in which people experience grief depend on factors such as their individual personality, cultural context, belief system and religious background. Other factors which may complicate feelings around bereavement and loss are instances which may constitute traumatic bereavement. These may be deaths that are seen as sudden, perhaps through murder, terrorism, activity of war, accident or suicide. It may be that the child was a part of events and is suffering from their own experiences of trauma as well as experiences of grief and loss.

In contrast, the death of a loved one may have been expected, and punctuated by frequent hospital admissions and physical separation from family as treatment was sought.

The death or loss of a family member can also present further challenges to a child's life. There may be implications for income, routines and housing. It is unlikely that we can consider bereavement and loss in isolation, as they touch on various aspects of a child's life.

Bereavement may be the result of the death of a parent, grandparent, sibling or other family member, as well as a friend and/or member of the wider school community. Some children will be particularly sensitive to the death of a pet even with the

DOI: 10.4324/9781003273110-10

understanding that a pet is likely to have a shorter expected lifespan than that of their human companions.

Bereavement in the context of schools is particularly important. There has been research which suggests that some children who have experienced bereavement experience long-term difficulties in relation to their loss.

Winston's Wish (2019) indicates that a child who has suffered a bereavement may not appear to be their typical self, citing some changes that you might see. I have used these changes, and added an additional column to list what you might see within the classroom and wider school setting:

Some changes	What you might see in school
Feelings of numbness	Not being able to concentrate or see the bigger picture in schoolwork
Loneliness	Not playing with friends
	No longer engaging in hobbies or interests
	Avoiding group work
Worries/anxieties about the rest of their family and whether they are safe	Frequent absence from school
	Behaviour which leads to suspensions to avoid being at school
Feelings of needing to be more responsible for the family	Engaging in activities that put them at risk of child criminal exploitation in terms of making money
	Frequent absence from school, as taking on more parental/nurturing duties in the home
Anger and rage about what has happened	Impulsivity
	Quick to anger and get into arguments with friends or teachers

(Continued)

Feelings of hopelessness; 'what is the point?'	Not completing homework or schoolwork
	Not engaging with previous hobbies
Somatic symptoms (feelings of sadness through the body, such as tummy upsets, headaches etc.)	Frequent absence from school
	Complaints of feeling sick or tired
	Lack of concentration
Absorption in own grief	Lack of concentration in class
	Tearfulness
	Avoiding others
	Not completing schoolwork or homework

Consider the following case studies and ask yourself: What feelings of loss, trauma and bereavement have the students experienced?

CASE STUDY 1

Student A lived at home with their mother. They had been a victim of domestic abuse and would frequently see their father physically hurt their mum. When they were 13 years old, they saw their dad strangle their mum. It was then that Student A telephoned the police, and they were moved to temporary housing. However, despite the move, Student A and their mum remained unsafe and Student A was followed home from school. Their dad entered the temporary housing and killed the mum, in front of Student A. Student A was a witness to the event and gave evidence against their dad in court. Student A now lives with their maternal grandparents 200 miles away from where they used to live. They have changed schools but still speak to some of their friends whilst trying to make new friends in the area.

CASE STUDY 2

Student B attends the local secondary school and is 15 years old. Their school is a fairly big one and there are several changes of classes throughout the day. In maths, Student B would sit next to Student C. On a Tuesday night Student B found out through social media that Student C was stabbed at a house party. By Wednesday, Student C had died from their injuries. There were lots of rumours at school about who had done it and what had happened. Student B wasn't very friendly with Student C, but would sometimes text them for help with homework. No one sits next to Student B in maths anymore, and Student B keeps thinking over and over again about how Student C didn't answer the text message to explain some of the classwork.

CASE STUDY 3

Student D is 13 years old and has lived with their foster parents since the age of 4. Student D had previously experienced neglect and emotional abuse from a young age before moving into the care of their foster parents. However, their foster dad started to become unwell and was diagnosed with leukaemia. Life at home changed dramatically with lots of visits to the hospital and the start of chemotherapy, and Student D no longer being met at the top of the road on the way back from school. After six months, Student D's foster dad was moved into a hospice for palliative care and died shortly afterwards.

CASE STUDY 4

Student E was ten years old when she was living in Afghanistan. Her family moved to the UK to escape from the conflict shortly afterwards when Student E was 11. Before then she had been made to leave her school as girls were no longer allowed to attend. Coming to the UK meant that she had left behind her grandparents as well as her friends. She started a new school but didn't speak any English. Student E had very little support in the community, having lived in temporary accommodation initially before moving to a permanent residence significantly farther away and therefore needing to change schools. She was not able to keep in contact with children from her previous school, as she didn't have the communication skills.

INTERVENTIONS AND STRATEGIES FOR BEREAVEMENT

Interventions and strategies for bereavement often sit within the context of wider school policy and external support. However, some things can be done to support the micro level of teacher or teaching assistant. Following are some suggestions to help you think creatively about how to support children who may be exhibiting SEMH needs as a consequence of bereavement. For those who are diagnosed with PTSD, I recommend reading Chapter 19 to deepen your understanding.

BEREAVEMENT TOOL 1: PROVIDING ROUTINES BUT ALLOWING FLEXIBILITY

Earlier, I highlighted that one of the difficulties of children in bereavement is struggling to complete schoolwork or homework. Whilst it is important to keep routines and high expectations of children, we must also caveat this with the understanding that the world as they know it has changed dramatically. Routines still remain important, as school can be the thing that links 'normality' and their future wishes. To help with this, you may wish to consider extending the date for which homework should be submitted, or providing additional support or scaffolding to complete schoolwork.

BEREAVEMENT TOOL 2: OPPORTUNITIES TO REMEMBER

Following the loss of a child or an adult within the school community, it can be helpful to provide opportunities for others to collectively remember. This should not be forced but optional moments that children can be part of in some way or another to mark their remembrance of someone from the school community. There are different ways that this can be done and I have provided some ideas. You can choose which will be most suitable for your school community, and you are likely to have your own ideas or be able to elicit ideas from the wider school community to make it as personable as possible.

- Plant flowers/trees in their memory.
- Create a bench with a plaque with their name and a quote that encapsulates them.
- Make memory jars which can be returned to regularly to add notes about the individual.
- Make a memorial book which individuals can sign and add photographs and the like.
- Paint rocks with pictures and memories of the individual.

BEREAVEMENT TOOL 3: OPPORTUNITIES TO DISTRACT

Thoughts and feelings around bereavement can be distressing and not conducive to the classroom setting. Providing a box of activities that a child can choose to engage with may be beneficial for them to feel grounded. Grounded in this context means slowing down thoughts and feelings and trying to be situated within the now rather than the past or the future. Whilst it is important to be able to experience those emotions, it might be that a sense of calmness can help the child in that moment when things feel overwhelming. Some activities are:

- Ask the child to name five things they see, four things they can touch, three things they can hear, two things they can smell and one thing they can taste.
- An activity box with things such as colouring, puzzles or sensory toys which are in low demand.
- A walk in the playground.
- Contributing to a memory activity as listed earlier.

SUMMARY

- Whilst grief and loss can be considered normal parts of life, it can affect individuals' mood, concentration and friendship groups.
- Bereavement and loss can have a long term effect on the individual.
- Bereavement and loss can be understood, in some instances, as traumatic and adverse childhood experience.

BIPOLAR DISORDER

Bipolar disorder is a formal mental health classification which is described in both the *International Statistical Classification of Diseases* and the *Diagnostic and Statistical Manual*. Bipolar is described as an episodic mood disorder – that being there will be periods of time when a young person may present without symptoms, and other times they may exhibit manic or depressive symptoms. Previously, bipolar was referred to as manic depression and this might be the phrase by which you are more familiar. Bipolar disorder is especially relevant in a resource for teachers working with adolescents, as its symptoms are most likely to develop between the ages of 15 and 19 (NHS, 2019).

Manic symptoms	Depressive symptoms
Euphoria	Less interest in things previously enjoyed
Irritability	Feeling worthless
Increased activity	Difficulty in concentration
Rapid speech	Feelings of guilt
Increased self-esteem	Changes in sleep
Grandiosity	Changes in appetite
Less need for sleep	Less energy
Impulsivity	Tiredness
Reckless behaviour	

There are several subcategories of bipolar disorder, with the most relevant to this book being referred to as type I and type II. Some types of bipolar disorder include the symptom of psychosis (please see Chapter 20 for a focus on psychosis), as well as rapid cycling (quickly moving from mania to depression than the

DOI: 10.4324/9781003273110-11

more typical representation of bipolar disorder). Whilst going into more specific details of bipolar disorder might be illuminating to the reader and of particular importance for clinicians, the focus of this book is to refer to how those in schools might support children who have SEMH. Rather than going down a more clinical pathway (which I am neither qualified nor experienced to do), I will focus on what tools and resources schools can use to support a child who is symptomatic of mania. For a child who is currently presenting as depressed, please refer to Chapter 12, which discusses depression in more depth for specific strategies that may be supportive during periods of low mood.

INTERVENTIONS AND SUPPORT FOR CHILDREN WITH BIPOLAR DISORDER

BIPOLAR DISORDER TOOL 1: KNOWING THE SIGNS

It is likely that be that some of the symptoms described earlier in relation to mania are at odds with school behaviour policies and general approaches to learning. For example, being irritable, impulsive and engaging in reckless behaviour are things that are likely to be very challenging within the classroom, not just for the young person displaying symptoms but teachers and other children. Knowing that these are symptoms will be important to help a teacher understand that the young person is not being intentionally disruptive or argumentative but is struggling. Therefore, knowing the signs of bipolar disorder and the particular way that a child may behave when becoming unwell will be vitally important to make sure there is no additional conflict or challenges for a child during periods of distress and, hopefully soon after, recovery. If the young person has a diagnosis of bipolar disorder, they have hopefully worked with a psychologist or another therapist on 'relapse prevention'. Relapse prevention is a psychological intervention which aims to recognise early warning signs of mania and depression (Pontin, Peters, Lobban, Rogers, & Morriss, 2009). This is often a part of psychoeducation, where a person is supported to understand what bipolar is, some of the signs of becoming unwell, and strategies and approaches to support during these periods. Knowing the signs for key staff in schools can be a really helpful way to make sure that staff approach a child with the lens of support rather than behaviour management. Next, is a resource that might be amended/adapted for the specific needs of a young person and provides ideas to help school staff know the signs.

My warning signs that happen **before** a period of mania:	The things I might do when I am **having** a manic episode:	The things that may **help** me are:
E.g. I find it difficult to sleep.	E.g. argue with teachers	E.g. go for a walk around the playground with a member of staff

BIPOLAR DISORDER TOOL 2: ACCOMMODATIONS FOR SIDE EFFECTS OF MEDICATION

A young person with a diagnosis of bipolar disorder may take medication to help with preventing a relapse and/or managing symptoms. In these instances, it is helpful for school staff to understand:

- the name of the medication
- when the medication is meant to be taken (especially if during the school day)
- the dosage
- what should happen if a dose is missed
- the side effects (and in particular what the young person experiences as side effects)

In knowing this information, the next step is to ensure that the appropriate accommodations are made to support the young person in fully taking part in school life without feeling like they have to continually ask or require special permission to do things that make it easier for them. There is a range of different medications for bipolar disorder, but some common side effects that may affect a young person are listed below, with associated common adjustments that may be made to ensure that the young person feels comfortable and supported to attend school. These adjustments should not be assumed but considered after a full discussion with the young person about what they would like and feel comfortable with.

Thirst	Water available to drink whenever required
	Use of toilet when needed throughout the day including during lessons
	Issue of a toilet pass to stop young person being stopped in hallways when expected to be in class
Hand tremors	Extra time to complete tasks
	Use of computer to type notes or to complete tasks
	Longer time to eat lunch and the offer of another space to eat lunch if wanted
	Use of digital alternatives for art
	Call upon the expertise of an occupational therapist for individual assessment and recommendations
Blurred vision	Notes on computer to allow for enlargement
	Consideration of seating plans for young person to be nearer to the teacher
	Use of audio to complement reading tasks (for example, 'talking books' or use of technology to read out information)
Tiredness	The school day modified, for example, later start time, early finish time or specific times to rest during the day
	Reduction of homework
Upset stomach	Unfettered access to the use of the toilet (see Thirst above)
	Allowance for eating snacks to settle stomach as required

BIPOLAR DISORDER TOOL 3: BREAKING DOWN TASKS

If a young person is finding it difficult to concentrate and complete tasks, consider approaches that you may more typically use for those with attention deficit hyperactivity disorder (ADHD). One of which is the breaking down of tasks so there are small achievable tasks during periods of concentration.

SUMMARY

- Bipolar disorder often develops between the ages of 15 and 19.
- Bipolar refers to 'highs' (mania) and 'lows' (depression) which are characteristic of the disorder.
- It is likely that bipolar disorder, when a person is symptomatic, will have a profound effect on their behaviour within school, in both their ability to concentrate on their learning and their relationships with peers.

10

CHILD CRIMINAL EXPLOITATION (CCE)

Child criminal exploitation (CCE) is defined as the coercion of a person under the age of 18 to embark on actions which are against the law. The Children's Society (2021) defines it specifically as:

> Another person or persons manipulate, deceived, coerce, or control the person to undertake activity which constitutes a criminal offence when the person is under the age of 18.

In England, whilst it is difficult to ascertain the true number of children who are victims of CCE, it is thought to be around 46,000 (The Children's Society, 2021). This represents a significant number of children being exploited, which is then likely to have their education, lives and families affected by the criminal acts of others.

Some adolescents are exploited through county lines. The term 'county lines' refers to drug trade routes within the UK that are separated by counties. It involves the suppliers of drugs who are based in larger cities and typically involved in organised crimes or gangs to develop their trade in other areas (Stone, 2018). This can mean that adolescents may miss school as they are set up in 'trap houses' to prepare to sell drugs. The Children's Society (2021) reports that 84% of parents they surveyed expressed concerns about county lines.

In policy direction, the term 'contextual safeguarding' was first used by the University of Bedfordshire to attempt to address harm that was beyond that of the family in 2015 (The Association of Directors of Children's Services Ltd., 2018).

DOI: 10.4324/9781003273110-12

However, despite several years, there has been little literature which details how it might be tackled and challenged within the school context.

During my research into this area, I conducted a literature search and found only one journal article which provided suggestions concerning this topic and how to support it within school (May, Kloess, & Hamilton-Giachritis, 2021). A specific toolkit I reviewed was published by The Children's Society (2018) and references how schools may pick up early indicators of CCE.

In the UK, the focus of CCE is a safeguarding response referred to as contextual safeguarding. Traditionally, safeguarding was about protecting a child from interfamilial harm, however, in more recent years there has been increased discussion about the potential harm from those around a child – from that of peer groups, older adults who wish to exploit children and their local community.

In terms of schooling, this can have a fundamental impact on a child's well-being. We can see that being at risk of extrafamilial harm may influence a child's behaviour and their other areas of need (drug use and abuse, trauma and so on). Whilst a multi-agency approach is called for, there is not enough understanding of how we might support children in the school environment around this complex issue.

One approach is by using the term CCE; this is to reaffirm that children are just that, children and should be protected from harm. Concerns around 'adultification', which places the emphasis on children making adult decisions and being treated as such, do not take into account children and adolescent development which may make them more likely to engage in risky behaviours without factoring in implications beyond the immediate.

In considering the risk factors relating to CCE, there is interplay between multiple vulnerabilities. These may include a child having already been a victim of physical and emotional abuse, a history of neglect, and episodes in which the child is missing from the care of a trusted adult (The Children's Society, 2018). Some generic advice is also offered in The

Children's Society toolkit. It emphasises the importance of involving the child in decision making as, by contrast, the coercive, unsafe adults who exploit them will not allow them to make their own choices.

The organisation Mentally Healthy Schools (n.d.) acknowledges the risk factors relating to CCE, including:

- attachment difficulties
- unstable family environments
- violence within the home
- a sibling or relative with a history of criminal behaviour
- frequent moves
- lack of adult supervision
- being discriminated against
- feelings of isolation
- no sense of belonging
- feeling unsafe

The information presented then provides a limited number of examples to support preventing and responding to CCE, these being understood that a young person being exploited is an outcome of their vulnerabilities, creating a culture where young people feel safe and supported, finding out and signposting different people young people can talk to if they are being exploited, and incorporating of health and well-being lessons to build self-esteem (Mentally Healthy Schools, n.d.). Using this as a guide, I have elucidated on the broader themes to provide some strategies that can sit alongside these themes to give different ideas to help school staff understand what CCE is and how it might be addressed within the school setting and wider community.

INTERVENTIONS AND STRATEGIES FOR CHILDREN AT RISK OF BEING CRIMINALLY EXPLOITED

CCE TOOL 1: UNDERSTANDING THE VULNERABILITIES AND PROFESSIONAL CURIOSITY

There is a range of available training that looks at issues around contextual safeguarding. These are likely to be offered to you locally by social care as well as organisations such as the University of Bedfordshire, which has specific research and resources into the areas of CCE (University of Bedfordshire, 2023). A way of understanding the vulnerabilities of young people in your school community is through incorporating training as part of the regular safeguarding focus.

It is vital that a whole-school approach is used, and this becomes challenging when considering the role of a classroom practitioner. However, acknowledging some of the potential signs of CCE and having a wider continuing professional development (CPD) might help with an overall culture of awareness and identification.

One approach for CPD is by using case studies (some examples are provided next) and asking staff to highlight what some of those vulnerabilities may be to elicit discussion and think of strategies and plans accordingly. Whilst I have omitted demographic details, the pastoral lead or CPD lead may wish to include more information to flesh out the case study and reflect your own school community.

CASE STUDY 1

Student F is 13 years of age. They have moved several times in the last few years after their mother, themselves and younger sisters were subjected to domestic violence from their dad. Some of those moves have included temporary accommodation offered by hostels before finally being housed several hundred miles away to escape the violence. This has meant that Student F no longer lives near their family, and that they feel sad that they don't really know anyone in the local area. Student F has low attendance to school but is often seen in the local area 'hanging around' and associating with others who are dealing cannabis.

CASE STUDY 2

Student G is 15 years old. They are a looked-after child after being neglected by their parents. They are currently living in a care home, after difficulties with finding a foster home. There have been several telephone calls to the police after Student G has damaged the care home, including smashing windows and breaking doors. Student G will often leave at night and sometimes not return to the care home for a number of days. During this time, they do not respond to text messages or telephone calls. When they return from these episodes, they won't say what they have been doing or where they have been. Instead, they go to their room and sleep for a few days before returning to school. When they are at school, they prove themselves to be intelligent, articulate and seem to enjoy school.

CASE STUDY 3

Student H is 14 years of age. Student H lives at home with both their parents and their older sister who is currently attending university. Student H's attendance at school seems to be positive. However, they've recently been suspended from school after there were concerns that they were vaping and had drugs on their person. However, they refused to be searched, so it was not clear if they did have anything on them. Whilst suspended from school, they were found to be on a train without paying the fare. They were asked to produce their ticket, but refused and hit the ticket inspector in the face. Running away, they were quickly stopped by the police and it was found that they had two bags of MDMA powder on their person.

CASE STUDY 4

Student I lives with their mum and dad. Their mum and dad are addicted to heroin and often ask their child to visit the dealer to bring back their drugs. Student I is now 15 years old and has been doing this since they were 10 years old. Student I sporadically attends school and is often late when they do. Student I always goes back home to their mum and dad, and has several caring responsibilities for them both.

Some questions you can ask of the preceding case studies include:

- What do you think are the risk factors relating to CCE?
- What strategies could you put in place as a school to help the student directly?
- What strategies could you put in place to help support the student's wider network?
- Which organisations or people in your wider network would you utilise to provide additional support?

There is a lack of consensus for a definition for the term 'professional curiosity' (Burton & Revell, 2017), although there are a number of attempts by safeguarding organisations to provide a broad understanding as part of their training and resource materials (Leeds Safeguarding Children Partnership, 2021; Manchester Safeguarding Partnership, 2023). For the purposes of this book, I define professional curiosity as that of respectful uncertainty and evaluating situations by taking into account a range of views and perspectives. It's about not being assumptive and really trying to develop a deeper understanding of just what might be seen on the surface. Using this definition, how would you apply professional curiosity to understand the case studies from a range of perspectives?

CCE TOOL 2: COMMUNICATION WITH MULTIDISCIPLINARY AND EXTERNAL TEAMS

It is noted that children with SEMH frequently need support from a range of sources beyond that of the school. These include local authorities as well as the health, social care and justice systems (Thompson, Tawell, & Daniels, 2021). Children who are being criminally exploited are more likely to require a multidisciplinary approach to support their needs.

An adolescent who is in school feels safer than a child who is out of school or not attending. Nonetheless, CCE may be felt within the school environment in a range of ways. For example, you might notice a decline in attendance, lack of interest in schoolwork or homework, or lateness in starting school. As a classroom practitioner, what you notice on a daily basis is vital, you are often the person who may see the child frequently and notice changes. As a member of staff within the school, your communication about friendship groups and how a young person is presenting is key information to others within the wider community. Reporting what you notice to the appropriate safeguarding and pastoral leads can make all the difference for someone else to be able to piece together what is happening and make links.

It might be that there are natural 'touchpoints' where you can explore your concerns with social care, child and adolescent mental health services (CAMHS), or police, but irrespective of this, ensuring that you effectively communicate and record decisions with the wider team around the child is vital.

It may be that you are not the person who can ensure that all of this happens, but you can ensure that your wider concerns are reported and recorded accordingly. You may have an appreciation that meetings with wider professionals will likely be scheduled and have an understanding of the remit of the group. You might want to have an understanding of which people are invited to such meetings, for what purpose and whether you should be included in attendance to provide information. You may notice that it is not just paid professionals that attend these meetings, but also those from the third sector may be included.

It is easy for a child at risk or actively being criminally exploited to be lost within lots of discussions and reflection without any real change. Disrupting the criminal activity around the child is key but so is making sure that the team around the child works together to make sure that a trauma-informed approach is also considered and how this may be driving challenging behaviour within the school.

CCE TOOL 3: FRIENDSHIP GROUPS

There are arguments that children who are more vulnerable to CCE are those who feel disconnected or disjointed from their peers. Whilst friendship groups may be a more familiar term with younger children, it is of value to consider how these may be incorporated with older children that still may require support to make and sustain friendships. This is especially important during periods of transition, such as when children are leaving their more familiar friendships with children in primary school and travelling farther afield to access secondary education, or perhaps when they are moving classes within school to specialise in certain subjects. All these things might offer further fragmentation in relationships. Friendships do not have to be named as such or be orientated around ideas of friendship; groups could be built upon mutual interests and hobbies. I would suggest that such groups cover a range of interests and hobbies to be as inclusive as possible. For example, whilst your school may take pride in its sports or perhaps its arts, to include a range of different topics led by an adult would give more opportunity for adolescents to try new things and develop skills in a range of areas outside of the typical curriculum.

SUMMARY

- Any adolescent is vulnerable to criminal exploitation depending on the wider context around them.
- CCE is not something that happens overnight but can be seen in the context of 'grooming', the time and investment in developing a 'trust' between victim and perpetrator.
- A child may not see themselves as a victim of exploitation, making it particularly challenging in supporting them.

11

CRIMINAL SEXUAL EXPLOITATION (CSE)

Criminal sexual exploitation (CSE) is a specific type of child sexual abuse and is defined by the Department for Education (2017) as

> where an individual or group takes advantage of an imbalance of power to coerce, manipulate or deceive a child or young person under the age of 18 into sexual activity (a) in exchange for something the victim needs or wants, and/or (b) for the financial advantage or increased status of the perpetrator or facilitator. The victim may have been sexually exploited even if the sexual activity appears consensual. Child sexual exploitation does not always involve physical contact; it can also occur through the use of technology.

Sadly, it is likely that if you work within safeguarding or pastoral support in schools or other settings you may have supported children who are victims of sexual exploitation. The inclusion of this topic in the context of SEMH is an important one. Children who are sexually exploited are more likely to suffer from post-traumatic stress disorder (PTSD), anxiety and depression, as well as being more vulnerable to self-harming or the use of drugs. In knowing about CSE and what may be some of the underlying needs, we can hopefully be in a position in which we can help children.

The first part of helping children who are victims of CSE is understanding what it is, and then how it affects them individually along with their peers and the wider school community.

DOI: 10.4324/9781003273110-13

Clearly, the priority must be to stop the sexual exploitation, protect those children and stop them from experiencing any more harm. This must be from a multidisciplinary approach which involves police agencies, social care, schools and mental health services. It is likely that from your own perspective, you may add other third-sector agencies. Worryingly, one of the repeated issues detailed in serious case reviews (SCRs) is health professionals' poor understanding of CSE and how they might be able to safeguard against it (Mason-Jones & Loggie, 2020). As CSE requires a coordinated approach, the more we read, find out and apply professional curiosity, the better position we are in to support the victims of CSE.

There have been several high-profile examples of criminal sexual exploitation within areas of the UK, and these were brought to the attention of a number of agencies, without necessarily due regard, curiosity or understanding of the gravitas of the situation. Often children discussed in SCRs have had extensive and repeated contact with statutory services, with many recognised as having SEND. Some of the SEND relate to SEMH needs, while others relate to communication and interaction. The young people's attendance at school was also noted to be irregular (Griffiths, n.d.). It is notable in the SCR that school is mentioned several times as repeatedly bringing up concerns, working with families as well as the children directly to try and influence change within the wider community. As with many safeguarding reviews, a key component when children and young people are let down is the lack of connection with the relevant agencies. None of the tools that I outline next should be seen as isolated acts, but as developing strategic touchpoints where information is shared robustly, consistently and coherently.

The importance of including CSE within the context of resources relating to SEMH may seem like an odd one, but it is noteworthy that CSE has huge negative implications on a child's emotional and mental health, as well as their physical health. This can lead to a long-term health impact which can contribute to early death through suicide or murder (Mason-Jones & Loggie, 2020). If there is an opportunity to prevent this and support a child, then I want to take that moment to reflect. Key learning features of an SCR are indicated to be:

- early recognition
- timely referrals
- action from the above

(Mason-Jones & Loggie, 2020)

Thus these feature in the following sections to support key staff within schools to consider some approaches where they might be enacted.

INTERVENTIONS AND STRATEGIES FOR CHILDREN AT RISK OF CSE

CSE TOOL 1: NOTICE

Knowing what CSE is and understanding the potential signs of CSE is a vital step in supporting children who are victims of such abuse. It is important in that without knowing the signs of CSE, then you are unlikely to be in a position in which you are able to report your concerns, draw in the support of others or support with interventions. As this book has been written in the UK, there is specific guidance to understanding some of the signs of CSE, but there are likely to be situated within the wider cultural context of being in the UK. Other countries likely have their own guidance and understanding to draw upon. Next, I have included examples of external behaviour that may indicate, from the UK perspective, that there is CSE:

- being in receipt of money, jewellery, technology or new clothes without a reasonable explanation (for example beyond what you may expect at birthdays, Christmas, or within the context of a family's situation)
- associated with others who are known to be in gangs
- being isolated from their normal peer and social groups
- unexplained absence from school

- going missing from home or not arriving home until late or leaving home without saying where they are going
- being secretive about whom they are receiving messages or phone calls from
- coming home drunk or under the influence of drugs
- having a sexually transmitted infection
- having relationships with those with more power or those that are older than they are
- signs of physical assault or hiding of bruises, cuts
- change in emotional well-being (withdrawn, quietness)

(adapted from Department for Education,
2017)

Following are different examples of children who are being exploited. The case studies can be used from a training perspective to help participants consider the potential signs of CSE and how they may utilise what they notice to be able to report to the relevant organisations or key members of staff who have overall responsibility for safeguarding. You may wish to write your own examples of children who are being exploited (being mindful about confidentiality) or utilise other SCRs and draw out information from those to open critical discussion about this topic. These case studies have drawn upon information from SCRs and other material (CB, 2015; Department for Education, 2017)

CASE STUDY 1

Student J is 15 years of age. They have recently been getting in trouble at school. Quite low level at first – forgetting their pen – but then not completing homework. They are looking tired throughout the day, and you notice that irrespective of the weather they cover their arms and legs with jumpers and tights. They have not been associating with their normal friends and have been reluctant to hand in their phone at the beginning of school as is part of the behavioural policy. Their attendance soon drops from previously over 90% to lower than 80% without real explanation from the parents. Sometimes Student J might come into school, register but then leave.

CASE STUDY 2

Student K is 13 years of age and there are repeated reports of them meeting with much older students from the local college after school. Student K is repeatedly getting into physical and verbal fights outside of school. Most recently, you have heard rumours from other students that Student K is engaged to a much older boy. You aren't sure how old the older person is, but you know that they are one of the other students that attend the local college, so at least 16 years of age.

CASE STUDY 3

Student L is 13 years of age. They have always been very quiet at school but more recently have refused to undress for PE and reports that they have sprained their ankle as an explanation of why they can't do sports. Student L is coming in late to school, with red eyes as if they have been crying or even perhaps taking drugs. They have begun to wear a lot of make-up in school and refuse to take it off. You know that there have been several instances of Student L being reported missing from home, not coming home at night and returning straight to school in the morning from wherever they have been the evening before.

REFLECTIVE QUESTIONS ABOUT THE CASE STUDIES

1. What do you think are some of the concerns detailed in the case studies?
2. What would you do if you noticed some of these behaviours?
3. Does your school have a specific person you could talk to about your concerns?
4. Would these concerns affect how you supported the student in class?

CSE TOOL 2: DEVELOPING SAFE RELATIONSHIPS

Young people who are sexually exploited are likely to feel hurt, embarrassed, angry and struggle to trust other adults. Developing safe relationships, where boundaries are clear but young people can express how they feel without being judged, is likely to be an area which is difficult but important for their well-being. Those who have experienced CSE say that being listened to, being believed and not being patronised is key within professional relationships (Lefevere, Hickle, & Lurcock, 2017). In order to support young people who are at risk of exploitation you may wish to draw upon the skills and expertise of people outside of school – this may be from the third sector, mentoring organisations or social services. It is important that due diligence is applied in terms of making sure those adults working with vulnerable children have undertaken the relevant training and safeguards to ensure they are an appropriate adult to work with children. You may wish to use pastoral staff within the school setting, as they will have more natural 'touchpoints' to see a child, and also not have to be so tied into a child's attendance to school which may have begun to be sporadic. How you develop these safe relationships is using the key ideas outlined earlier – *listened to, believed and not patronised.*

CSE TOOL 3: FOCUSSING ON WELL-BEING NOT JUST THE CLINICAL

Clinical support for children being sexually exploited is of course important; for example, it is vital that adolescents have access to treatment for sexually transmitted infections or their understanding of options concerning potential pregnancy. However, the focus on a young person's needs must be holistic, and on their emotional and mental health as well as their physical clinical needs. Thus, the multidisciplinary approach is key to making sure children have access to a key adult to be able to speak to about their experiences. It might not be that they are ready for specific therapeutic input but be better served by a safe adult who they can talk to about some key issues that are affecting them.

SUMMARY

- CSE is a specific type of child abuse and should be considered as such. Terms such as 'child prostitution' are not just out of date but harmful, as they place blame for abuse on the child.
- Children's emotional needs must be considered as important as their clinical needs
- An adolescent who is being exploited sexually is likely to have some difficulties that may also mean you refer to other aspects of this book (for example, CCE, depression, anxiety or PTSD).

12

DEPRESSION

Clinical depression is beyond that of feeling 'sad' or feeling low. Clinical depression is a medical diagnosis which can have a significant impact on a child's well-being, their ability to concentrate, to feel motivated and, for some, to attend school at all. To meet the criteria for depression, the young person will have at least five of the symptoms from the following list. Further, within the same two-week period at least either (a) depressed mood and/or (b) loss of pleasure must be present.

The symptoms of depression are:

- feeling depressed for most of the day and for most days
- loss of interest in things that they previously may have enjoyed
- weight loss or weight gain with associated changes in appetite
- slow thoughts (poverty of thought) and decrease in movement
- feelings of tiredness and not having enough energy
- poor self-esteem or feelings of guilt for most days
- difficulties in concentration or not being able to make a decision most days
- reoccurring feelings of death, or thinking of suicide, with or without a plan to undertake suicide

We can see from reviewing the diagnostic criteria of depression how it might have a fundamental impact on being able to function, let alone thrive, within the school community. Depression may also co-exist with other difficulties and challenges such as anxiety, self-harm, suicidal ideation, eating disorders and low

DOI: 10.4324/9781003273110-14

self-esteem. These can also provide difficulties in focussing, concentrating and being present within the classroom environment. Every person with depression will present differently. Whilst some children may appear 'fine', their mood, thoughts and feelings may make it hard to enjoy the things they did previously. For others, they may 'get through the day' but find it difficult when they get home to be able to enjoy things and may distance themselves from their typical friendship groups.

INTERVENTIONS AND STRATEGIES FOR DEPRESSION

Unfortunately, there is little evidence that school-based interventions for depression are sustainable, although they may work post-intervention from a clinician (Edwards, 2021; Gee et al., 2020). This can seem quite discouraging considering the opening paragraph about interventions and strategies for depression. However, holding on to the hope presented after initial clinical support, I offer ideas that may not be sustainable but may be initially supportive to an adolescent after a period of distress.

DEPRESSION TOOL 1: THINK OF ALTERNATIVES

As described earlier, depression is often punctuated by low mood, motivation and engagement in things previously enjoyed. There is often a 'warming up' period where things are more difficult in the morning, from getting up, getting out of bed and getting dressed. Coupled with the potential for an individual having a poor night's sleep, it is unsurprising that a young person may find it hard to attend, engage and be enthusiastic within the school environment. To support a child as some of the interventions are put in place, such as cognitive behavioural therapy (CBT) or medication, considering alternatives to timetables may help. For example, if a young person finds it hard to get up in the morning, look at using a staggered start time to help accommodate. Or to build motivation, look at their previous interests to see if there can be careful attention to helping them attend a club available within the school environment.

DEPRESSION TOOL 2: CHECKING ON MOOD

Moods change throughout the day, as well as throughout longer periods of weeks and months. Sometimes changes can seem very subtle and not immediately obvious. Checking on mood could be as simple as touching base with a key adult in the morning as well as a quick check-in before they leave school. Some children may not tell you verbally and would prefer to keep a mood diary which they can show someone how they are feeling without necessarily having to converse on it.

Within the context of class, the use of signs can be a helpful way to subtly communicate how they are feeling without necessarily verbalising it. This can be done in various ways and I would recommend doing this after discussion with the child. Some options include:

- coloured wristbands associated with the traffic light system (red for immediate support, amber for keep an eye on me, green for I am okay)
- emoticons or symbols on a piece of paper on the desk
- coloured pages at the back of the homework diary using the traffic light system

DEPRESSION TOOL 3: CONSIDER THE EFFECT ON COGNITION AND ADAPT ACCORDINGLY

Depression can have a fundamental effect on a child's cognition; this could be the way they are able to think through things and process information as well as motivation to engage in a task. Having this knowledge means that you are likely to want to be able to adapt your teaching instruction to support a child to be able to participate in class. Approaches can include things such as scaffolding a task so that it is broken down into several steps; this way the child might not be overwhelmed by the end task. You can present this in a way that children can tick off what they have done to promote a sense of achievement as well as keep a record of what they have done to be able to pick up the next lesson.

What I need to do	Tick when done
Read through pages 16–19	✓
Highlight the key words (up to 5)	
Write out the definition of those key words	
Using all the key words explain the term 'oxbow lake'	

SUMMARY

- Depression can affect an individual's thought processing and concentration, reduce physical movement, and cause weight loss or gain.
- Depression is likely to affect school life as well as outside interests and enjoyment.
- Clinical depression lasts beyond two weeks and therefore is not just moments of low mood.
- Not all children will be able to share their thoughts and feelings with others.

DRUG USE AND ABUSE

You may have heard the term 'public health approach' to supporting children (or adults) who smoke, take drugs or drink alcohol excessively. The public health approach refers to a multidisciplinary approach which aims to promote the health, well-being and safety of a population (Centers for Disease Control and Prevention, 2022). This approach has four distinct stages that are particularly relevant to the use of drugs by young people:

1. Define and monitor the problem
2. Identify risk and protective factors
3. Develop and test prevention strategies
4. Assess which strategies are effective and adopt them more widely

(adapted from Centers for Disease Control and Prevention, 2022)

The public health approach cannot be done in isolation; it is not the role of one pastoral team, one school or even a group of schools but it must also include that of health services, social care, youth offending team and wider community members such as religious organisations, youth groups and other third-sector organisations.

Harm reduction interventions are more targeted to meet the needs of a specific group of people who are engaged in what is seen as risk behaviours. These will typically employ the public health approach as highlighted earlier but be more focussed on an explicit group of individuals (Hickle & Hallett, 2016). For example, it might be that it is acknowledged through research

DOI: 10.4324/9781003273110-15

and data that young people who have a history of being victims of domestic violence, or a certain age group or have repeated suspensions from school may be more likely to be exposed to illegal drugs. A harm reduction approach would look at how to support those specific groups of young people to minimise their risk of using or exposure to certain events.

INTERVENTIONS AND STRATEGIES FOR DRUG USE AND ABUSE

In support of the aforementioned factors, I recognise the need to encompass an approach which focusses on harm reduction rather than punitive measures. This can be specifically challenging for the schooling community, which may have specific concerns about the use of drugs within and outside of their school. Ensuring that there is a focus on drawing upon the expertise of others and sharing concerns within the wider community is important. For example, it might be that there are issues in an area around particular use of drugs, where they are purchased or how they may be moving around the area. This topic of drug use should also be considered with child criminal exploitation (Chapter 10), as well as drawing upon interventions and strategies to consider the underlying reason for children using drugs in the first place (for example, depression or anxiety).

DRUG USE AND ABUSE TOOL 1: A WHOLE-SCHOOL APPROACH

A whole-school approach looks at educating children about the risks associated with drug use, as well as an understanding that adolescents may likely have curiosity surrounding the use of drugs. They may also have been exposed to others using drugs, perhaps their parents or friends, as well as on television or social media. Being able to provide them with material that clearly explains the risks is a way to at least ensure that if children use drugs they have all the relevant information at hand and are not basing their decision on misinformation, rumour and hearsay. Some schools opt to provide this information via one-off assemblies. I think there are dangers in this route, especially if the children most in need to access information happen to be absent that day or just not paying attention in the first place. Whilst assemblies may be helpful as a jumping-off point for discussion, I recommend seeking someone who talks from experience. This may be a person that has a previous history of the use of drugs or sale of drugs. A word of warning of this approach: ensure that the person talking does not glamourise the use of drugs, but provides an honest oversight of (hopefully) their previous decision-making. This should also be followed up with support around access to information where children can have a range of resources such as information sheets about different drug types, their legality or otherwise, and the potential consequences of use.

This literature should be freely available in different parts of the school site where other information is stored so that children do not feel 'exposed' in seeking the information out. Further, by adopting a whole-school approach, some schools in the UK have access to school nurses. The role of the school nurse is diverse and their exact approach is likely to differ depending on the remit of the school. Their role includes the promotion of good health and improving the health and well-being of children. They will be excellent resources to draw upon for school staff, children and their families around the use and misuse of drugs.

DRUG USE AND ABUSE TOOL 2: EMPLOYING THE PUBLIC HEALTH APPROACH

Many older children have used drugs, and as a school community, you are unlikely to know to what extent, either how frequently or which type of drugs. The employment of a public health approach recognises that children may use drugs and how best to support harm reduction. Using publicly available data, we can get a glimpse into some of the national trends. For example, for those seeking support, cannabis remains the most frequently used drug cited with 80% of young people seeking treatment reporting its use (The Office for National Statistics, 2022). The same report reviews those accessing treatment, with two-thirds being boys. This is important information, as it helps us understand where we might focus more targeted support. However, questions and context should also be applied to our own settings. It might be, for example, that more boys are likely to seek treatment for the misuse of drugs, whilst girls may just as frequently use drugs but not seek help. Further, the data does not delve deeper into children that may identify as different to their birth sex (for example, are those young people who are trans male or trans female more or less likely to seek treatment for drug use than their peers).

Finally, the data suggest that referral routes into treatment programmes differ enormously. A quarter of referrals into national treatment programmes in the UK are referred by the youth justice system, whilst just below that is mainstream education which represents 19%. Even less are health and substance misuse services (The Office for National Statistics, 2022). Taking this into account – that many children will not seek support – we can see that schools are spaces in which many children might have access to professionals who can signpost and support.

For many children, you can use a universal approach that supports the whole-school community in being able to understand the broad implications and risks of drug use. Much of this is done in assemblies as well as within personal, social, health and economic (PSHE) classes. However, there are dangers with this method, especially assembly. First, you cannot guarantee the levels of concentration of those attending assembly, that is if those who most need the support will attend at all. Second, in the open forum, it might be difficult for children who may already be using drugs to feel that there is an authenticity with those delivering the programmes. Linked to my earlier recommendation, many schools use external speakers who have a previous history of drug use (and subsequent abstinence) to tell their own stories. I remember from my own schooling history that the parent of a child who died from the use of ecstasy visited our school in assembly and took questions. Considering it was over 20 years ago, there is something to be said about the longevity of the message.

Considering that children may need more specialised support, schools in the UK may have access to school nurses who can support with work around reducing the risk of drug use. School nurses can also signpost children to more specific links to organisations that can do more focussed work on drug use. They can also help support teaching staff in the planning and delivery of PSHE.

SUMMARY

- Whilst drug use may present particular challenges to the schooling environment relating to discipline, a more supportive approach to use is the employment of a public health approach.
- The use of data to understand your local area and national picture may help you in planning and organising support.
- Those that use drugs may have other difficulties (for example, anxiety, depression, psychosis), which means that referring to other chapters of this book becomes important.

14

EATING DISORDERS

The term 'eating disorders' refers to a group of psychological disorders which affect an individual's intake of food. Eating disorders include the more well-known disorders such as anorexia nervosa and bulimia, and the less spoken about binge eating disorder (International Classification of Diseases, n.d.). Eating disorder refers to the distinct behaviour around the consumption of food. Accompanying this is often a significant preoccupation or distress about body weight and physical shape (Watson & Lask, n.d.).

ANOREXIA NERVOSA

Anorexia nervosa is the severe restriction of intake of food, which leads to significantly low body weight in relation to a person's age and sex, and has an enormous impact on their physical health. This is coupled with an intense fear of weight gain despite being underweight. Those with anorexia nervosa will have a disturbed view of their body weight and appearance (American Psychiatric Association, 2013).

There are several features of anorexia nervosa that are likely to have an impact on a child's functioning within school, separate from that of the physical manifestations of the lack of food intake. Children with anorexia nervosa will likely have:

- poor self-esteem
- low mood
- feelings of anxiety beyond that of food
- concerns about the school uniform and how they present to others
- self-harm beyond lack of food intake
- the need to have rigid daily routines

DOI: 10.4324/9781003273110-16

In addition to the psychological features of anorexia nervosa, low food intake may also impact cognitive functioning (Tenconi et al., 2021). These difficulties may include:

- the ability to make decisions
- memories about the self being altered; for example, some memories may feel very strong, others weaker (referred to as autobiographical memory)
- executive function including:
  - working memory
  - flexible thinking
  - regulating emotions
  - following instructions

Both difficulty with executive functioning and autobiographical memories may continue even after clinical recovery. This may mean that whilst schools may expect a child to be fully recovered after they have been discharged from hospital and seemingly on the road to recovery, some of the difficulties will exist after the stages of more significant intervention. This is important to remember when planning and supporting children upon their return to school. Intervention and support for a child are likely to include ensuring meal plans are followed, consideration around homework, as well as support within the class that does not contribute to poor self-esteem.

AVOIDANT/RESTRICTIVE FOOD INTAKE DISORDER (ARFID)

Avoidant/restrictive food intake disorder (ARFID) has similar symptoms to anorexia but without the addition of having disturbances of how the person views/experiences their body. Symptoms include severe restriction of the intake of food, which leads to significant weight loss because of nutrition deficiencies. Those with ARFID will require either nutritional supplements or even feeding directly through the intestine or nasal gastric tubing, and their ability to function both psychologically and socially will be impaired (American Psychiatric Association, 2013). Previously ARFID was referred to as 'feeding disorder of infancy or early childhood' and symptoms had to be evident before the age of six years old. However, the age requirement has been removed from the current *Diagnostic and Statistical Manual of Mental Disorders (DSM-5)*, which explains its inclusion in this resource book for older children.

Due to the specific requirements of enteral feeding (enteral feeding is a medical term which refers to the intake of food directly through the gastrointestinal tract), further consideration in school will likely be made on how this may be administered in a safe way where children can lead as full a school life as possible and feel confident in how they wear their school uniform and ensure effective hygiene relating to the medical equipment. Also, appropriate risk assessments should be conducted with family and medical personnel.

BULIMIA NERVOSA

Bulimia nervosa is characterised by recurrent periods in which a person may binge eat. This is where during a short period (and it is noted in the *DSM-5* to be within two hours) a person may eat a significantly larger amount of food than what a typical individual may consume otherwise. A person will have a feeling of being unable to control or stop how much they are eating. In order to compensate for this food intake, they will respond with behaviour to prevent weight gain. This may be through intentional vomiting, using laxatives, fasting in between these episodes or excessively exercising (American Psychiatric Association, 2013)

As with anorexia nervosa, girls are more likely to be diagnosed and affected by bulimia nervosa (Striegel-Moore, 2009). However, it is important to remember that whilst this may be the case, you may also have boys who are also diagnosed with bulimia. Children with bulimia nervosa are likely to have several difficulties in school. These include:

- feelings of low self-esteem
- presenting as defiant and stubborn

- self-harm beyond that of binge/purging
- variable mood

(Watson & Lask, n.d.)

Depending on the level of weight loss and malnutrition, young people may also have the difficulties outlined earlier in relation to cognition and learning.

BINGE EATING

The criteria for binge eating disorder include repeated and persistent periods of binge eating, which includes eating large amounts of food when you are not hungry, feeling guilty and embarrassed about how much has been eaten, and eating more quickly and feeling uncomfortably full. Those who binge eat will have feelings of being distressed. Unlike bulimia, there are no compensatory behaviours of purging afterwards (American Psychiatric Association, 2013).

Whilst we see anorexia nervosa and bulimia nervosa as being more serious than binge eating, binge eating can have a huge impact on a young person's life and their behaviour within the school environment. Whilst bulimia nervosa includes purging (such as inducing vomiting or the use of laxatives), binge eating may not. However, it is likely to include feelings of guilt and self-hatred after a binge eating episode.

INTERVENTIONS AND STRATEGIES FOR EATING DISORDERS

EATING DISORDER TOOL 1: KNOWING THE SIGNS

Knowing the signs of an eating disorder goes beyond that of the diagnostic criteria. The UK eating disorder organisation Beat (2023) lists signs that those in a schooling environment may notice and which may indicate an eating disorder. Wider signs may range from fluctuations in weight, complaints of feeling cold and comments of being fat (Mental Health First Aid International, 2020). Working with adolescents in the secondary school setting means that staff may not see these signs consistently due to subject timetabling, and some changes may not be pathological (i.e. diagnosable mental health conditions) but instead are throwaway comments around self-esteem and other changes notable within typical puberty. To help, I have listed different examples of behaviour you may witness within the schooling setting, but also encourage those of you who have concerns to liaise with parents/carers as well as seek further training to continue to develop understanding.

Some signs of an eating disorder you may notice within the schooling environment:

Weight changes (fluctuations, increase, decrease)	Extreme neatness	Feelings of tiredness
Eating on their own (avoiding the dining room, missing lunch, bringing own food)	Finding it hard to concentrate	Being irritable
Perfectionism (for example, repeatedly doing homework, not being satisfied with work)	Increasingly isolated	Micrographia (small handwriting) (Murali, Jon, & Palmer, 2010; Beumont, 1971)

EATING DISORDER TOOL 2: CONSIDER HOW TO SUPPORT EXECUTIVE FUNCTIONING

As discussed earlier, children with eating disorders (except for binge eating) are likely to lose weight and not have a sufficient level of nutritional intake. This can affect processing, thinking, concentration and attention. With discussion and liaison with family and medical personnel, consider lowering demands for things outside of school such as homework and instead offer opportunities to review work in class. You can also 'chunk up' work rather than presenting more complex questions or pieces of work. For example, providing children with a page of script from a book or a play for analysis rather than the whole text-book. This will mean that they are practising the core skill that you would like them to without being overwhelmed and distracted by a larger text.

EATING DISORDER TOOL 3: UNDERSTANDING THE JOURNEY TOWARDS RECOVERY

Each journey of recovery or 'living with' an eating disorder is different, however, there are trends that suggest that eating disorders may last longer than other mental health conditions and have a deeper impact on a person's physical health needs. There are also ups and downs, or, in other words, relapses. It might be that any plans or interventions need to be returned to support a child during periods of an acute phase of being unwell. Understanding the bigger picture of recovery may help by enabling those within the school to recognise that recovery from an eating disorder can be a long process. It may be that the child is unable to physically attend school, as there may be a need to reduce physical demands. In these instances, consider the use of technology to include children; this can include innovative telepresence technology, filming of lessons or just clear class notes to help an individual know they have not missed out when physically unable to come to class.

SUMMARY

- Some of the after-effects of eating disorders may last longer than the initial presentation of the illness.
- Eating disorders can affect a person's emotional and mental health well-being, as well as their physical and therefore their cognitive functioning.
- Eating disorders often take a long recovery period, and young people require extensive support during this period.

15

HARMFUL SEXUAL BEHAVIOUR (HSB)

Harmful sexual behaviour is a complex area where the child is likely to be a victim as well as a perpetrator of difficult behaviour. The behaviour is likely to contravene the social norms of the school community as well as possibly being illegal and dangerous. Further complexities are also acknowledged with the potential that there may be overlaps with other difficulties relating to child sexual exploitation (CSE) and child criminal exploitation (CCE).

There have been different terms associated with HSB as well as definitions which characterise behaviours that might be *inappropriate, problematic abusive and/or violent*. To this end, Hackett (2014) has produced a continuum of HSB that is likely to be a useful tool in understanding whether behaviours presented might be seen within the context of HSB.

DOI: 10.4324/9781003273110-17

Normal	Inappropriate	Problematic	Abusive	Violent
• Developmentally expected • Socially acceptable • Mutual, with consent and reciprocated • Shared decision-making	• A single incident of sexual behaviour that doesn't constitute 'normal'	• Developmentally unusual and socially unexpected • No overt elements of victimisation • Unclear around consent • May lack reciprocity • Unequal power • May include levels of compulsivity	• Victimising intent or outcome • Includes misuse of power • Coercion and force to ensure victim compliance • Intrusive, informed consent lacking or not able to be freely given by victim • May include elements of expressive violence	• Physically violent • Highly intrusive • Instrumental violence which is physiologically and/or sexually arousing to the perpetrator • Sadism

The continuum of HSB begins with people observing behaviour, and having an understanding of what is typical, normal and developmentally appropriate. This is reliant on professionals' wider understanding of children's typical development, the implications of puberty and how young people may interact socially.

Hackett's continuum is helpful in that it begins to unpick issues concerning the potential of escalation of behaviour, as well as seeing how some presentations of behaviour may include examples from different columns. To understand whether the behaviour can be seen as HSB, there needs to be wider consideration of the:

- young person's chronological age
- young person's developmental age (for example, maturity, learning disability, broader understanding)
- power dynamics
- intention of act(s)
- whether there is CCE or CSE by someone beyond their normal peer group influencing behaviour

It is no surprise that with the increasing use of technology, there are additional ways in which young people can exhibit HSB. HSB can include recording and distributing pornographic material as well as coercing individuals to behave in certain ways with threats to widen this distribution to the wider intended audience. Some of the latter issues may be addressed within specific assemblies, personal health and social education, as well as safety discussions in information and computer technology classes. However, I do not know of any evidence which clarifies how useful these generic and broad approaches are with young people that may already be exhibiting HSB. Moreover, the focus tends to be on the victim's response and protection of self rather than a specific way of changing the behaviour of the perpetrator. There likely needs to be specific, targeted and multidisciplinary targeted approaches that cater to the individual. It may also be that the behaviours exhibited are at the extreme end of the continuum, making it particularly difficult to be able to mitigate risk within the wider school setting, which by its nature will have younger children and/or those who may have additional vulnerabilities.

TECHNOLOGY-ASSISTED HARMFUL SEXUAL BEHAVIOUR

The use of the internet and social media remains a concern for professionals and parents. It would be amiss when considering HSB exhibited by young people to not consider the role of technology within its presentation. The children you work with and support will likely have significant access to technology, which may be an additional driver to HSB. One definition of technology-assisted HSB is as follows:

> One or more children engaging in sexual discussions or acts – using the internet and/or any image-creating/ sharing or communication device – which is considered inappropriate and/or harmful given their age or stage of development. This behaviour falls on a continuum of severity from the use of pornography to online child sexual abuse.
>
> *(Hollis & Belton, 2017)*

In a review of children and young people who used the service Turn the Page (2023), it was acknowledged that 46% of them that exhibited harmful sexual behaviour used technology to further assist their HSB. It was unusual for children to only engage in technology-assisted HSB (Hollis & Belton, 2017, p. 31). Examples of technologist-assisted HSB include the following:

- developmentally inappropriate use of pornography
- the making, taking and distribution of indecent images of children
- sexting (which includes making images of themselves as well as sexual content via text or other mobile phone chat programmes)
- inciting sexual activity
- sexual harassment of others

- attempts to groom others
- exposing other children to pornography

Some of the access to pornography would likely be seen as extreme and/or illegal pornographic material.

 HARMFUL SEXUAL BEHAVIOUR TOOL 1:
TRAINING FOR KEY SCHOOL STAFF

When explaining key aspects of HSB, I acknowledge the complexities of understanding the topic. Training is therefore a vital component and tool for supporting children in the school community who might both be victims as well as perpetrators of HSB. To begin, consider your safeguarding/child protection policy and who might be the staff members who may be informed that such behaviour could be occurring within the school community. They will likely need specific training in the following:

- typical sexual behaviour of adolescents
- the use of technology that may influence behaviour
- how to access local support
- what constitutes harmful sexual behaviour

Training is a key aspect which needs to be considered; you may seek training from the local area as well as national organisations to make sure that school staff are aware of what would constitute typical adolescent behaviour before understanding what may be identified as, inappropriate, problematic, abusive or violent. Another approach to support with training is to engage with your local community and, within the realms of confidentiality, share experiences, interventions and outcomes. Consider what was effective, which agencies helped and how did they find out about the HSB. You can develop this even further by sharing and discussing serious case reviews published on the National Society for the Prevention of Cruelty to Children (NSPCC) website to find out if there are any learning opportunities for you as a school or the wider organisations you work with to develop better working practices.

HARMFUL SEXUAL BEHAVIOUR TOOL 2: COMMUNICATION WITH MULTIDISCIPLINARY TEAM AND BEYOND SCHOOLS

In working successfully with children with HSB we mustn't rely on just the expertise within the school environment but broaden out to other relevant organisations. In the UK there are a number of long-standing organisations that may be of help which are referred to at the end of this book in Further Resources. However, please ensure that due diligence is made in regard to safeguarding any organisation that you utilise or draw upon expertise by asking the following questions:

- What are the individual's professional credentials?
- Does the individual have access to clinical supervision?
- Is it mandatory or best practice that they are regulated by a specific healthcare professional association? If yes, are they registered with the appropriate body? In the UK, organisations include:
    - Health and Care Professions Council
    - British Psychological Society
    - General Medical Council
- What are the intended outcomes of engaging with the external agency? For example:
    - assessment of need
    - individual intervention
    - broader understanding of family context
    - development of robust risk assessment

HARMFUL SEXUAL BEHAVIOUR TOOL 3: SEXUAL HARM RISK ASSESSMENT

I acknowledge that talking about harmful sexual behaviour in children can be distressing for adults and children alike. It may be that talking about personal acts is uncomfortable, feels like a violation of privacy and is against our own sense of personal conduct. However, to be able to write a sexual harm risk assessment, here are a few tips that may help:

- undertake the appropriate training
- understand the nature of the child's needs
- use the correct language rather than euphemisms or vague terms such as 'inappropriate' to describe acts that are concerning

Risk management plan

What are the child's strengths?	This is an important aspect to help understand the 'hook' to support a child in engaging in more prosocial behaviour. Are they good at drawing, crafts, computer games? Do they really like maths or can they tell you a myriad of history facts? It is important that when considering risk that there is also the balance in helping a child feel like they belong to the wider school community.
What have been the incidents or behaviours that are worrying/ problematic?	What has been noticed or observed? This might be things that have been said, behaviour or things that have been reported. When/if behaviour was addressed, what was the response by the child or young person? How did parents/carers or the wider network respond when incident was reported?
Are there other behaviour concerns outside the context of HSB?	For example, has a child been violent, are they disruptive, do they leave class or threaten to hurt other children?
Does the school have specific concerns?	Are there particular children who are being targeted? Are there concerns about others within the family home? Are there aspects of behaviour that need to be discussed to understand the wider context?

(Continued)

Who is at risk of harm?	Consider age, groups, gender or particular vulnerabilities/SEND of children that may be targeted.
Are there any specific locations that are particularly risky?	For example, toilets, particularly quiet or unobserved parts of the playground, changing areas. Consider how this might be managed in terms of additional staffing, opening up/exposing specific spaces.
Does the child engage in other risky activities?	The wider context is very important and can help understand how to mitigate risk and further support the child and others around them. Is the child supervised when using the internet or social media? Do they have access to drugs or alcohol?

SUMMARY

- When dealing with harmful sexual behaviour, there must be a coordinated approach among different organisations/disciplines.
- You must remember the potential victim (or actual victims) of behaviour as well as those who perpetuate harmful sexual behaviour.
- It is likely that those exhibiting harmful sexual behaviour are also victims themselves.

16

EMERGING PERSONALITY
DISORDER

I will start with a very clear principle: children cannot be diagnosed with a personality disorder. However, I have seen in the last few years the term 'emerging personality disorder' being used within education, health and care plans; social care documents; and other associated materials as an attempt to describe behaviours from children who may have experienced significant trauma and distress in their younger years. As emerging personality disorder is not a diagnosis, there is no real statistical data I can rely on, so instead I can say anecdotally that a number of children who have suffered from neglect, trauma, abuse or fractured relationships may be referred to as having an emerging personality disorder to attempt to explain some of the behaviours of, for example, repeating disruptive relationships, self-harm, anxiety and depression.

The diagnosis of having a personality disorder for adults has helped some in being able to navigate support and understand how they interact with the world and those around them. For others, a personality disorder diagnosis has not supported their understanding of some of the difficulties they have faced. There is still a significant stigma to the term personality disorder, and although this might be a really helpful discussion generally, it is not one for this book.

If you want to find out more about personality disorder as you are working with a child that has been identified as likely to be on the trajectory of diagnosis once an adult, I have signposted some resources at the end of the book.

You may have heard individuals refer to complex trauma when attempting to provide a framework to understand

DOI: 10.4324/9781003273110-18

children's behaviour that may be challenging. Complex trauma refers to when a person is repeatedly exposed to traumatic events of a similar nature, such as that which may be physical, sexual or emotional abuse (Brooks, 2019, p. 18). These are likely the very same children who may be referred to as having an emerging personality disorder.

 ## EMERGING PERSONALITY DISORDER TOOL l: TRAUMA INFORMED

The development of a child is dependent not just on biological factors but also on their social environment. It is no surprise then that beliefs about the self are shaped by those around them. Siegal (1999) recognises that for those who already believe they are in some way bad, punishing them through "impress[ing] on them the 'badness' of what they have done only confirms their inner view of themselves" (also see Brooks, 2019). There is the further suggestion that a child's 'window of tolerance', what they are able to endure in terms of stress, is likely to be smaller than that of those who have not experienced trauma (Siegal, 1999). That is not to say that we ignore behaviour that is deemed unacceptable in the classroom and wider school environment, but we use a trauma-informed approach to be able to ensure that we do not cause *additional* harm to children who are already struggling. That is because punishment is unlikely to be effective (remember these children already know that they are 'bad') and being punitive rather than supportive does little to demonstrate that parents can be safe people.

EMERGING PERSONALITY DISORDER TOOL 2: SAFE WAYS TO EXPRESS EMOTIONS

Having opportunities to identify and express emotions in a safe way is important for those who have experienced trauma to be able to experience heightened emotions without resorting to activities such as self-harm. This is not an overnight approach; this is something that requires time, commitment and consistency. The first approach is for children to be able to recognise that they are finding things difficult. One way is by providing opportunities in which they can touch base with an adult. I have found this works best at specific points during the day, i.e. morning, at lunchtime and the end of the day. The timings of these may be reduced to just morning and afternoon, especially in the context of busy schools, and nor do they need to be long in themselves. It can simply be saying "Just checking in to see how you are doing", as well as a debrief at the end of the day, "How do you think today went?" As schools are busy places, they are likely relying on one person to do this, setting things up to fail. I would suggest having several people who are available to do this but with a similar approach and style. This will mean that if a person is absent, then another person can make sure this happens.

The next step is to listen carefully to what a child responds with, not only what they say, but their tone and intonation. If they say "I'm fine", is this congruent with their tone and body language? Take seriously how a child responds; not just their words but their demeanour too. There is likely to be a time when they tell you they are feeling down or sad or angry, and perhaps want to report something that has happened during the day. You may not be able to deal with the situation immediately, but make time during the school day to return to them; tell them when you will see them and set a time to go through it properly. Ensure that you share this openly with them with phrases such as:

- "What you have said is important, and I want to listen. Can I meet you again at lunchtime in my office so we can have somewhere quiet to speak?"
- "That sounds like a difficult day. Is there anything we can do to make sure that doesn't happen again tomorrow?"
- "This sounds upsetting. What happened next?"
- "It sounds like you becoming angry. Do you think there is a different way this could have been dealt with?"

SUMMARY

- You cannot diagnose a person under 18 years of age with a personality disorder.
- There is significant debate on the diagnosis of a person with personality disorder and whether it should be understood within the context of complex trauma.
- The trauma-informed approach is a vital component in supporting those who may have experienced trauma but do not have a diagnosis of post-traumatic stress disorder (PTSD).
- Relationships and how you talk to an individual are key.

SELF-HARM

'Self-harm' is a term to describe deliberate acts by an individual which aim to harm, hurt, cause injury, pain or poison themselves. There may or may not be intent to end life. Whilst intentional acts of injury to oneself may be under-reported, there are suggestions that 17% of adolescents self-harm with the average start of behaviours being between the ages of 12 and 13 (Crudgington & Ougrin, 2022). For those who self-harm, it may be something that they keep intensely private or try to explain by suggesting that the injuries were caused by something else. Wanting to stop may be very different to being able to stop, with self-harm being understood in the context of trying to manage and minimise distress relating to difficult thoughts and feelings (Papyrus, n.d.).

In 2022, the National Institute for Health and Care Excellence (NICE) issued draft guidelines on self-harm which included the role of schools and personnel on how to support children. In the guidance, NICE sets out a number of things that schools should do to support children and young people who self-harm including:

- having policies and procedures in place which outline how to identify self-harming behaviour and what to do in response
- having a designated lead for implementation of policy and practice relating to self-harm
- how to reduce the distress of both the young person who self-harms as well as their peers

INTERVENTIONS AND SUPPORT FOR
CHILDREN WHO SELF-HARM

SELF-HARM TOOL 1: DISTRACTION

Some children may have moved to habitually self-harming or to the requirement to use their hands for something positive.

DOI: 10.4324/9781003273110-19

As you are working with older children, it might be that they need a more focussed distraction to prevent self-harming. For some, colouring, playing or listening to music, or crocheting can be effective. However, it must be noted that there is limited evidence on how effective distraction is in preventing self-harming, and I recommend talking with both the child and their parents/carers to see if it is helpful for their particular circumstances.

SELF-HARM TOOL 2: CONVERSATION PROMPTS

Talking to children who self-harm can be very difficult; we might have our own particular experiences or be embarrassed about talking about self-harm. We might be fearful that we can distress someone even further. Self-harm is an emotional subject and can be upsetting for all those involved – for the individual child as well as those who may witness self-harm or the after-effects. There are a range of feelings which might be experienced, such as guilt, shame, anger and sadness. Next, I include some examples of conversation prompts which can help open up conversation whilst not shaming the child and reiterating safeguarding responsibilities.

- "If I am worried about you, I can't keep what you tell me a secret and may have to tell other people to keep you safe."
- "Thank you for telling me about this; it must have been really hard. One of my important jobs, as well as teaching you, is to keep you safe. It might be hard to tell your parents about this, but can we do it together with Mr Smith?"
- "Is there anything we can do to help you feel safe?"
- "Is there anything happening that makes things more difficult for you?"

These conversation prompts don't take into account your own style of communication, your knowledge of a child or other factors. They should therefore be amended considering these factors with the intent of an open conversation and active listening remaining the same.

SELF-HARM TOOL 3: PROVIDING A SAFE SPACE

Leaving children alone when they are in distress is unlikely to be a sensible idea. It may increase their risk and further their vulnerabilities. For this reason, I have often been in a position when knowing that I am working with children who self-harm who are not allowed to use the toilet without express permission. Some even have their bags checked for equipment that they might use for self-harm. On other occasions, we have not just had to search bags but the perimeter around the school in the case of self-harm instruments being left around school grounds. This can feel incredibly counterintuitive. We want to make sure that we give children options and the ability to explore their emotions. However, we also have a duty to safeguard children and ensure that do not come to harm. Therefore, in providing a safe space, this should be discussed prior to the times when an individual may feel the need to self-harm. Identify a place within the school environment where a young person can sit and be without access to equipment that they may use to harm. For younger children, we might be talking about safety tents or reading corners. However, these are unlikely to be used by older students. Instead, consider with the child spaces they recognise as being calming and safe and a place where they might be seen but still feel is private. This could be a library, a pastoral support room or other particular space within the schooling environment. Ensure that this space has access to the resources required to maintain those feelings of safety.

SUMMARY

- In this book, deliberate self-harm is considered as separate from self-injurious behaviour, which may be more related to autistic spectrum condition.
- Self-harm is distressing for both the individual as well as those who are aware of it.
- Self-harm likely co-occurs with other difficulties such as depression or anxiety.

18

OBSESSIVE-COMPULSIVE DISORDER (OCD)

Obsessive-compulsive disorder (OCD) is an anxiety disorder that includes both obsessions and/or compulsions. In the case of OCD, there is the specific diagnosis requirement of recurrent and persistent thoughts, urges or images. At some point, these persistent thoughts will be intrusive or unwanted, and in most of those children affected, will cause anxiety or distress.

Compulsive behaviours will include things that are repeated and may typically be things such as frequent handwashing, ordering of items or checking things (such as whether a light has been turned off, a door closed and so on). In the context of school, you might see the repeated rubbing out of work, repeatedly rewriting activities or perhaps frequent visits to the toilet for handwashing.

However, you may not see compulsions, as these can also be carried out internally. For example, counting items, saying words in their head, or even retelling stories so there are different outcomes. These compulsions are done in response to an obsession or an internal rule that an individual is committed to.

The purpose of the compulsions, whether they are physical behaviours or mental acts, is to:

- prevent distress
- reduce distress
- stop an event or situation that may occur

DOI: 10.4324/9781003273110-20

These behaviours or acts are unlikely to be connected in a realistic way to the prevention, reduction or stopping of the situation, or if connected will be excessive. Symptoms of OCD can have a significant impact on a young person's functioning within school, both in class and transitions from activities and social time. In a 2013 study of 151 children, the most reported issue was that of concentrating on schoolwork and completing homework (Piacentini, Bergman, Keller, & McCracken, 2013). Further to this, a complicating factor when trying to support those with OCD is that students are likely to try to hide their symptoms from those around them (Leninger, Dyches, Prater, & Heath, 2010).

CASE STUDY

Student M is a 15-year-old girl with a diagnosis of OCD. Student M is dropped off and picked up from school. They are often late to class, and as they walk past classroom doors, they have to look in the reflection of the glass. You have noticed that Student M will often walk backwards to seemingly recheck themselves in the mirror before walking forwards again. This can mean that a journey from one classroom to another can take longer. It can also make it difficult for transitions for other children who are going to class as Student M will walk backwards as well as forwards without checking what is behind them.

INTERVENTIONS AND SUPPORT FOR CHILDREN WITH OCD

OCD TOOL 1: FINDING OUT MORE

Without knowing some of the information behind the obsessions and compulsions it can be hard to think of approaches that may support a child to engage in school life. It may also be difficult in that the young person may not want to tell you or be unable to. Lots of young people with OCD may feel embarrassed or scared by their thoughts and not want to share these with others. Being mindful of this is key to ensuring that you are not intrusive.

Thus, when trying to find out more to make reasonable adjustments, it needs to be taken on a case-by-case basis on whether it would be more beneficial to speak to a parent/carer, medical professional, support worker or the child themselves. This discussion can be part of a wider individual support plan or, if appropriate, ad hoc conversations to try to build a better understanding. Next, I have listed some questions you can use to try to find out more. These questions can be written down or asked verbally, once again depending on the relationship with the young person and their ability to be able to articulate their difficulties:

- Are there things before school that make it difficult to start on time?
- Can you think of ways that OCD impacts upon you at school?
- Is there anything you think we can do to make things simpler for you?

OCD TOOL 2: ADAPTATION TO SCHOOL TIMES

The snapshot of Student M's symptoms of OCD can be understood in the context of the physical expression of internal struggles. Our role within school is to consider how we might draw upon the expertise of others, but we can also look at strategies to support Student M directly in their successful attendance at school. Whilst for the school culture the establishment of rules and routines may be seen as important, it's clear that reasonable adjustments are an important mechanism for which to ensure that Student M is successfully part of school life. To this end, consider adjustment to school times including staggering starting and learning time, whether or not there is scope for Student M to stay within the same classroom to minimise movement between one space to another and speaking to Student M directly to see what accommodations may be made to support them directly.

OCD TOOL 3: PROVIDING INFORMATION IN DIFFERENT FORMATS

Distractibility and difficulty following teacher instruction are possible when a person is engaging in OCD rituals. It is unsurprising that in the fast-paced nature of a lesson, especially when preparing for examinations, that content and teacher input may be missed. An approach that can be helpful would be to provide information in different formats so that if there is a moment of distraction within the class, the student can return to a piece of content to review what they have missed, or even to reaffirm that they have not missed class content. This may be as simple as referring a textbook or an online video, or highlighting key notes on a worksheet.

OCD TOOL 4: THINKING THROUGH UNIVERSAL MESSAGES

It is commonplace for universal messages such as those relating to health, substance misuse, drugs and friendships to be conveyed during assemblies or lessons. To support children with OCD, consider how these messages may be understood within the context of an individual with OCD. For many of the children listening to these messages, they will herald a warning, but for some, they will play on an individual's mind and even form part of their obsessive thinking (Wells, 2006). Wider consideration of wider universal messages and how these may be interpreted by the individual, and having more direct work may be helpful ways in which to support a young person in acknowledging some of the challenging messages.

SUMMARY

- Compulsions can either be behaviours (things you might see) or mental acts.
- OCD can have a fundamental effect on a child's functioning at school, from their ability to get to school on time to attending classes to completing work.
- A child may be embarrassed about the symptoms of OCD and not share this with others around them. Sensitivity is required to be non-judgmental, and try not to force an individual to explain their thinking if they are uncomfortable.

19

POST-TRAUMATIC STRESS DISORDER (PTSD)

Post-traumatic stress disorder (PTSD) is a disorder that marks a specific and significant response after a traumatic event or traumatic period. This may emanate from one-off events such as involvement in or witness to a terrorist attack, assault or car accident, or perhaps more regular occasions such as being a victim of domestic violence, bullying or war. Both children and adults can experience and be diagnosed with PTSD, although for children the threshold (the number of symptoms) is less than that of an adult. The following criteria need to be included:

- The young person has experienced a traumatic event, which may be a death, near-death or physical threat to themselves or others.
- The person's response to this involved them feeling intensely fearful or helpless or horrified.
- The event is re-experienced via recurrent, intrusive or distressing memories of the event. This may be through images or thoughts.
- The event can be experienced through reoccurring dreams of the situation.
- Feeling as if the trauma is repeating.
- Avoiding things that may remind one of the trauma.
- Difficulty in being able to remember the trauma.
- Attempts to avoid the location of the trauma.
- Finding it hard to fall asleep, feelings of anger, difficulty concentrating and being extra vigilant to potential threats of harm.

(adapted from American Psychiatric Association, 2013)

DOI: 10.4324/9781003273110-21

CASE STUDY

Student N was on the bus going home from secondary school. They were positioned at the front of the bus when the bus came to a sharp stop. The front of the windscreen was cracked and they hadn't seen it but had found out very quickly the bus had hit a mum whose child had run out into the road. Whilst it was clear the mum was injured and required hospitalisation, the child was not hit. Student N did not find out whether or not the mum had lived as there were no other discussions about the accident. In the months afterwards, Student N has had repeated nightmares where they have seen the child and the mum hitting the windscreen. The images have also been coming to them in the classroom, making it difficult to concentrate. They keep on getting these thoughts and find they become really tearful. Student N finds that they can't get on the bus anymore and instead decides to walk home even though it takes them an extra 30 minutes. Student N is not only finding it difficult to sleep at night but also getting up in the morning because they feel so tired.

QUESTIONS TO ASK YOURSELF

- Is there any evidence in the case study that suggests that the child needs more support?
- What do you think are the implications of Student N finding it difficult to sleep at night?
- What strategies do you think you can put in place to support Student N within the classroom setting?

PTSD INTERVENTION AND SUPPORT

PTSD TOOL NUMBER 1: CONSIDER THE EFFECTS OF PTSD

In the case study of Student N, I highlighted the difficulty sleeping that they had and the knock-on effect of getting to school on time. Having due consideration to the effects of PTSD is a helpful approach in ensuring that the child doesn't feel punished for feelings that they are unable to control. Working with them directly, and the wider network (such as a parent or clinician), look at some of the effects of their PTSD that they feel able to express and make reasonable adjustments to support. For example, requiring a later start or time to rest may be a perfectly reasonable way to include a young person without it being onerous on planning or resources.

PTSD TOOL NUMBER 2: SCHOOL-BASED COUNSELLING AND PSYCHOSOCIAL EDUCATION

Interventions of school-based counselling can be a way in which to support children who have a diagnosis of PTSD, especially in instances where the PTSD emanates from a shared experience of a traumatic event within the local community. There is (sadly) a body of evidence from the United States of America and Palestine where children are likely to have been exposed to trauma (such as Hurricane Katrina or exposure to conflict) that details the efficacy of school-based counselling as having a positive effect of reducing symptoms of PTSD (El-Khodari & Samara, 2020). Moreover, educating children about the nature of trauma has been shown to help reduce somatic (the feelings in the body) symptoms of trauma, and help children understand more about their behaviours and feelings (El-Khodari & Samara, 2020).

SUMMARY

- PTSD is a distinct medical diagnosis and should not be conflated with trauma, adverse childhood experiences or attachment styles.
- The threshold for the diagnosis of PTSD for children is lower than that of adults.
- Not every child that has a traumatic experience develops PTSD.

PSYCHOSIS

Psychosis is when a person's thoughts and perceptions of reality are disturbed, and an individual has difficulty in being able to distinguish between reality. There are a range of symptoms of psychosis, and these include:

- false beliefs (delusions)
- hallucinations (seeing or hearing things that other people do not)
- incoherent speech

(National Institute of Mental Health, 2022)

Psychosis may emanate from the use of hallucinogenic drugs, or conditions such as bipolar disorder or schizophrenia. At times, psychosis can be part of depression, although this is less typical. You may notice that children respond to things that aren't there in several different ways. They may appear distracted, physically respond to what they are seeing or they may verbally reply to the voices they are hearing. Some children may stop eating food because they are concerned that others have interfered with what has been cooked. Other children may be concerned that they are being controlled by others or that they are being spied on. Adolescents may also be tired, as their sleep may be interrupted, find it hard to sustain friendships and find it hard to concentrate. You may be less familiar with psychosis, and how it presents can be quite difficult to understand. I will explain some of the key aspects of the diagnosis to help teachers gain a deeper understanding of some of the needs they may see in the schooling environment and to appreciate some of the challenges that adolescents may have during an acute phase

DOI: 10.4324/9781003273110-22

of psychosis. Psychosis can be very difficult for a young person in the school environment, but even when they do not have florid symptoms of psychosis (meaning having the full symptoms), such as during recovery, they may still experience aftereffects of medication that could affect them as well as the lower level symptoms as described earlier. To further help, I provide case studies to exemplify the description of how psychosis may affect the individual.

DELUSIONS

A delusion is when an individual has a belief in something that is untrue. This is the rigid belief that is likely to affect their everyday actions. There are different types of delusions that you may have heard of, namely, persecutory delusions and grandiose delusions. Persecutory delusions refer to one's conviction that someone or something is trying to hurt them.

CASE STUDY 1: PERSECUTORY DELUSIONS

Student O was attending school when they began to stop eating lunch. They insisted on bringing their own lunch to school. They began to lose weight and at first, you thought perhaps there were issues with how they viewed their body weight. However, soon this stopped, and you noticed they weren't eating food at all. You also noticed they were less interested in how they looked. Phoning home, you found out from the parents that Student O is also struggling with their eating habits at home. Previously, Student O would eat cereal for breakfast but now they were insisting on mini individual packs of cereal without any milk. Student O wouldn't offer an explanation of this, but their parents had found their diary which had lots of pictures they had drawn which seemed to depict someone pouring poison into their food.

CASE STUDY 2: GRANDIOSE DELUSIONS

In class you were studying a particular theme of music when Student P explained that they were related to the singer of the music that was being studied. You were surprised by this, as they had never mentioned it before. Student P went on to explain that they see them every Sunday, and had only just seen them this Sunday. You know this not to be true, as the person in question was currently touring overseas. However, you didn't think Student P was being 'silly' but really believed it. The other children in the class laughed it off, but you decided to telephone home to find out what you already thought: that this relation to the singer is not true. Talking to Student P's parents, they further expressed concerns about some of the things that their child were saying, including that they had special powers relating to music because of their close relationship with the artist.

HALLUCINATIONS

Hallucinations are where a person may experience things that other people do not. As with the general senses, people may experience these things by what they see, hear, smell, taste or even feel. Next, I provide some examples before further exploring them within the case studies to contextualise them within the schooling environment. Please note that olfactory and gustatory hallucinations are more unusual than visual, auditory and tactile disturbances.

Sense	Description	Examples
Visual	An individual may see certain people, animals, colours or shapes	The sight of wolves chasing an individual People watching them from their room Clowns participating in circus tricks nearby

(Continued)

Auditory	The hearing of voices or sounds around them	The sound of an incessant washing machine The voices of people talking to them
Tactile	Experience of being touched or feeling of others breathing or in some way physically connecting with the individual without any physical stimulus	Thinking that insects are crawling over their skin The sensation of the skin being burned Being touched sexually or having sex
Olfactory	Being able to smell things where there doesn't appear to be a cause of that smell and doesn't have a neurological cause	The smell of burning hair or faecal matter Food not smelling 'correct' or as expected The smell of flowers or perfume
Gustatory	The taste of something when there is no obvious cause (such as a dental issues, or residue food items)	The taste of metal or something bitter in the mouth

CASE STUDY 3: HALLUCINATIONS (VISUAL AND AUDITORY)

Student Q was a regular attendee of school and was otherwise a diligent and quiet student. However, you noticed that they stopped attending your classes. You didn't understand why, as they appeared to enjoy your class. Upon checking you found out that they were registering in the morning but very quickly would 'disappear' from the classroom. Bizarrely, one day you opened up the school administration office and found them sitting on the floor. You asked if they were okay and what they were doing.

"I am hiding," came the reply.
"Hiding from what?" you asked.
"The police. There are police outside and they've told us to hide."

CASE STUDY 4: HALLUCINATIONS (OLFACTORY)

Student R was sitting outside of the dining room where they were meant to be eating their lunch. You asked them to go and queue up inside and stop loitering.

"No way miss, it stinks in there. Someone has done a poo and it absolutely reeks." Confused, but thinking that perhaps someone had had an accident, you go into the dining room but notice no smell and no one responding. You go to speak to one of Student R's friends and ask them what has happened.

"Nothing. Student R keeps on saying the same thing about it smelling of poo but I don't know what they are going on about."

INCOHERENT SPEECH

Typically, when we have conversations with individuals we are able to follow what they are trying to say, and infer meaning and respond. There are instances where children may have speech and language needs, and when talking about 'incoherent speech' this does not refer to those children. We are referring more to the young people who previously did not have difficulty with maintaining a particular line of thought which is then translated into making their meaning understood. Those with disorganised speech may speak in ways where they don't answer questions from others, may say things that appear out of context, muddle their words or frequently change their topic of conversation. You might notice that they mix up their words and it becomes impossible to be able to elucidate meaning from what they are saying (referred to as 'word salad').

INTERVENTIONS AND SUPPORT FOR PSYCHOSIS

PSYCHOSIS TOOL 1: MAKING SCHOOL A SAFE SPACE

Having false beliefs and hallucinations can be very scary for an individual. They might not know what is happening and feel suspicious about the things that are happening around them or be suspicious of the intent of others. It is important to note that children with psychosis may feel unsafe, scared and in an acute phase of being unwell that they may not be able to attend school. However, as a child recovers, starting to build up their confidence in being at school will be vital. They may have worries about how to explain their absence, how to let others know (if they decide to) what they have experienced and feel embarrassed about their behaviour. Making school a safe space again takes time, so liaison with the child directly as well as those around them. Consider the lessons that they felt more confident in, the spaces in which they felt they belong and the friends that they have key relationships with. Alongside the young person, come up with a transition plan in returning to school that takes into account that attending full time initially may be impossible but instead incorporate a step-by-step approach to making school a safe space again for them.

PSYCHOSIS TOOL 2: CONSIDERING THE EFFECTS OF MEDICATION

Rather than repeating a large chunk from the section on medication for bipolar disorder, refer to "Bipolar disorder tool 2" (Chapter 9) to consider how medication to reduce the symptoms of psychosis may affect the individual. To reaffirm, consider the side effects for the individual; how these might be accommodated within school; and know who to liaise with around dosage, side effects and how to provide the medication safely.

SUMMARY

- Psychosis refers to a range of individual experiences, such as seeing/hearing or feeling things that other people do not.
- Psychosis is believing in things without evidence (for example, that someone is poisoning their food or has put a microchip in their brain).
- Psychosis may be caused by a range of things, such as an underlying medical condition (e.g. schizophrenia or specific types of bipolar disorder), the aftereffects of using hallucinogenic drugs or inflammation of the brain caused by an infection.

FURTHER RESOURCES

Within education, social care and the justice system there are a range of resources that may be helpful when developing your own techniques. In this chapter, I explore how you might go about mapping out your support networks to help you further. We can only support children in schools if we also have the support of others around us. I also use this as an opportunity to signpost resources that I have used or referred to which I've found particularly helpful in my practice when working with older children who have SEMH.

WORKING WITH PARENTS/CARERS

The biggest resource as a teacher or anyone working in the classroom setting is the people directly around you. Parents/carers are individuals who are likely to (a) know their child best (b) have their best interests at heart and (c) experience their child in most settings. One phrase that I am guilty of using is "they aren't like that at school", which negates the experience of the adult in the home setting. We all know that how we are in the home setting compared to work or other external settings can be very different. Being able to work with parents with children who have SEMH can be challenging, not because the parents/carers are challenging, but because they may have had poor experiences of education themselves, repeated the stories about their children too many times to count, and fought and struggled to get the support they need for their children. It is vital to try to be different to their previous experiences which may have been poor or lacklustre. That is not to blame other individuals or cast aspersions about their practice – we all work within the finite resources that we have – but it is to realise that

DOI: 10.4324/9781003273110-23

a person's journey in front of you at a meeting is just a small moment which may have been marked with rocky hills and frustrations beforehand.

This is not to say that working with parents/carers and the wider family is an easy task. In many 'customer-facing' roles, our interactions with the public are in passing, superficial and short-lived. Working in school environments is very different. Relationships with families may extend beyond that of the one child, with siblings attending the same school too. For those children with an education, health and care plan (EHCP) naming specialist, provision for this may be less likely, but this may provide challenges with an increased physical distance from the school and transition into placement at different points in the schooling year.

Secondary school also presents particular obstacles to developing relationships with families. Whilst at primary schools, parents/carers are likely to take children to school and pick them up, at secondary schools this is less likely to happen. Those natural touchpoints of quick chats at the school gate are unlikely to happen for an older child who travels independently to school. Instead, specific times are often allocated to debrief and report additional information about their child.

For some parents/carers, and especially those whose child has SEMH, these meetings can be daunting. We have already acknowledged in this book that children with SEMH are more likely to be excluded and suspended from school, and have poorer academic outcomes and lower attendance rates. Each one of these things gives rise to meetings in which parents/carers may feel targeted or blamed in some way. There is also the possibility that these meetings may be attended by external provisions such as social workers, youth offending teams, child and adolescent mental health services (CAMHS) professionals and so on.

Many parents/carers have also felt that they have had to fight to get the support that their child needs (and indeed may have a legal right to); these parents/carers may be considered as challenging.

> Such parents and carers are often described as 'challeng-
> ing' or 'difficult', but many have learned, through hard
> experience, that this is the only way to be noticed and to
> effect positive change for their children.
>
> *(Clements & George, 2023)*

There are also concerns that, when seeking support, those
children with SEND have been assessed with the lens of blame
rather than support. For example, when looking at issues concerning how institutions enact parent blame, 80% of social
workers were required to see a child's bedroom, this was irrespective of whether there were concerns or evidence pertain-
ing to abuse or neglect (Clements & Aiello, https://childhub.
org). This theme of blame is continued in this article, which also
expressed concerns that families were brought into processes
relating to child protection due to disagreements on how a child's
behaviour might be managed within the home setting (Clements
& Aiello, https://childhub.org).

Considering these challenges, there are different strategies
we can take to support the child in our schools. We also have
the power to do this irrespective of our roles within the school
community. Further, working effectively with parents/carers is
seen to benefit the child directly with their behaviour within the
school environment and beyond.

> Parent/carer engagement is important because work-
> ing together … has been shown to have a promising
> impact on the wellbeing, attendance, behaviour, sense of
> school belonging, intellectual development and attend-
> ance of children across a range of social and economic
> backgrounds.
>
> *(Mentally Healthy Schools, n.d.)*

STRATEGIES FOR WORKING WITH PARENTS/CARERS

WORKING WITH FAMILIES TOOL 1: WIDER SCHOOL CONTEXT

Next, I consider different ways that we might begin to look at
developing a culture and specific practical ideas when working

effectively with parents/carers. However, it must be recognised that having strategies which are not adaptive or flexible for your parental cohort will not be effective. You must also consider your school community and the myriad of nuances that make up your school setting.

Key area to address	Different strategies to help	Potential pitfalls
Parents knowing staff members	Noticeboard with information on staff Use of website which is up to date with key staff members Introduction letters when new staff join community and information when they leave Opportunities to meet staff prior to parent/carer evening, such as informal coffee mornings Events at different points during the day which allow staff and parents/carers to meet; this could be exhibition of artwork, coffee mornings or more formalised events such as parent/carer meetings	Secondary schools may have fewer face-to-face visits by parents/carers to school Some parents/carers may not have unfettered access to internet Some parents/carers may have lower literacy skills or English is not their primary language Childcare issues may present particular challenges to attendances Work and family schedules might make it difficult for many to attend

(Continued)

Effective communication	Consider use of email as well as telephone Contact parents/carers before issuing 'praise calls', or send positive postcards home as an informal way of building relationships Regularly send newsletters home Use translators and interpreters as necessary	Some parents/carers may have lower literacy skills or English is not their primary language
Enabling parents/carers to voice their ideas and opinions	Feedback forms Email or contact forms for parents/carers to feedback Signposting to SEND parental forums	Parents/carers not feeling listened to Parents/carers not having the required literacy skills to be able to utilise feedback forms or contact forms Parents/carers being disengaged
Developing parental skills in supporting children	Use of parenting programmes to guide a parent where there might be challenges across the home and school setting	Parental blame That parents need to feel that this is a supportive mechanism Groups need to reflect the community in which you work

(Continued)

	Library resources for parents/carers where they can 'check out' books that they feel are relevant	
	Specific groups which cover key topics, such as use of social networking sites, digital literacy of parents/carers, resources in the community, exam stress, supporting your child with anxiety	
Making physical environment a positive space	Have a walk-through of your physical environment	When doing your walk-through you may not see some of the challenges that parents/carers have in visiting your school. Consider approaching parents/carers to do the walk-through and report back to governors about their experiences.
	Is it friendly? Is it accessible? Have you considered that some parents/carers may have limited mobility, or use of prams? Are parents/carers warmly welcomed? Are they offered a drink?	

WORKING WITH FAMILIES TOOL 2: OPENING UP CONVERSATIONS

Beyond the wider school culture and strategies, I have also considered ways in which individual teachers may better develop relationships with parents/carers. I will start with a situation I found myself in several years ago. I share this personal story to highlight that we are all in a position in which we can learn and develop our practice.

I had been working in education for 15 years when I worked with a year 7 student with an EHCP, diagnosis of autism spectrum condition (ASC) with the recognition of anxiety and a pathological demand avoidance (PDA) profile. The pupil had had a period of elective home education (EHE) after continual inability to attend school. Their mum, when they came to visit the provision I was overseeing at the time, had explained that the student had real challenges in the home environment. But now they had an EHCP and she wanted her child to get used to the school environment as much as possible before secondary. The pupil was making age-related progress in all subject areas. As this was the case, I encouraged the pupil to attend mainstream classes as well as those within the specialised unit. The mum had telephoned me to say that she thought it would be too much for her child and that it would cause anxiety. I said to the mum, "They're fine at school".

The next day the student did not attend. Instead, I received a phone call from their mum, who asked me to listen to her child in the background. I could hear screaming, shouting and the throwing of items. The mum explained that she was safe as was her child. I immediately apologised and realised how unhelpful the phrase "they're fine at school" was.

In sharing this anecdote from my teaching past, I acknowledge that it is unlikely that was the first time I used the phrase "they're fine at school", but I realised in that stark moment how unhelpful it was. Rather than being supportive and reassuring, which was certainly my intention, it was actually belittling the parent's and child's experience and did little to change anything for them.

Next, I offer some alternatives to "they're fine at school" that teachers may wish to use on a one-to-one basis to help them think about different ways to approach conversations with parents/carers when there are difficulties. The focus of each phrase is to open up conversation as well as reaffirm parents/carers as experts of their children's lives.

You mentioned that they are [anxious, angry, upset]. Can you tell me what that looks like?

I am finding it difficult to support [name of child] in my class. Is there anything I could try that might help?

I understand that [child's name] is finding it difficult to [listen/ concentrate/focus]. Is there anything that you do at home that works that I could try?

How does [child's name] feel about coming to school and how do they show that?

What do you think could help?

Can you tell me more what is happening at home?

I've tried [name some examples], but these don't seem to be helping. Is there anything you recommend I could try that I've not yet?

I know that children often behave quite differently at home and at school. Do you think that might be the case here?

I've noticed that [child's name] doesn't appear [happy/ settled/comfortable] in class. Do you think that is the case?

Do you need any support?

OTHER RESOURCES

Author/ organisation	Title/URL	Type of resource
Mental health conditions		
Cathy Creswell and Lucy Willetts	*Overcoming Your Child's Fears and Worries*	Self-help guide
Dr Tina Rae	*A Toolbox of Wellbeing Understanding & Supporting Children & Young People with Emotionally Based School Avoidance (EBSA)*	Books
Association for Child and Adolescent Mental Health	www.acamh.org/	Website
Place2Be	www.place2be.org.uk/	Website
Young Minds	www.youngminds.org.uk/	Website
Bereavement		
Winston's Wish	www.winstonswish.org/	Website
Sarah Johnson	www.phoenixgrouphq.com/tools	Website
Child Bereavement UK	www.childbereavementuk.org/	Website
Dr Tina Rae	*The Bereavement Book: Activities to Support Children and Young People Through Grief and Loss*	Book
Emotional regulation		
Amanda Peddle	*TAM's Journey: The Beginning* *TAM's Journey: The Middle* *TAM's Journey: The End?*	Storybooks

(Continued)

Sarah Johnson	www.phoenixgrouphq.com/tools	Website
Harmful sexual behaviour		
National Society for the Prevention of Cruelty to Children (NSPCC)	www.nspcc.org.uk/	Website
Barnado's	www.barnardos.org.uk/	Website
Stop It Now!	www.stopitnow.org.uk/	Website
Brook	www.brook.org.uk/	Website

MAPPING SCHOOL SUPPORT

As a fundamental approach, it is important to consider the support and key individuals in your own local context. The resources (whether these are people, tools, community spaces or otherwise) are particular to specific contexts and can't necessarily be signposted within the context of a book with a wide audience.

Using the following as a framework, consider the individuals or organisations that you may draw upon to help you further develop your offerings for children with SEMH. Consider whom you might add to the bullet points.

Universal support – the support available for all children throughout your organisation

- *For example, teachers*

Targeted support – the support that is available for individuals or groups that require some more support

- *For example, specific lessons on emotional regulation*

Specialised support – the specific support that is needed for individuals or small groups that require more focussed attention to have their needs met

- *For example, counselling, mentoring programme*

Beyond the school gates is likely to be additional resources. Throughout the book, I hope to have reiterated the role of parents/carers as well as the young people themselves, but depending on your context you may have access to third-sector resources (charity, grassroots organisations) as well as relevant businesses. However, in mapping out this information, it is important to find basic information about these organisations to ensure that their values and visions match your moral compass.

Some questions that might help you:

- How is the organisation funded?
- What are the values of the organisation?
- How are staff/volunteers recruited and do they align with safeguarding/child protection?
- Does the organisation support all children or young people, or are there exceptions?
- What are these exceptions and what is the justification for them?

Finally, consider some of the references pointed to throughout this book. From the beginning it is important to have a broad overview of child development; how children learn and grow can be a fundamental way of understanding how we can teach to their age and stage in a way that ensures that children feel and are safe. This may be explored through storytelling, specific training or growing your own professional learning network through face-to-face opportunities or perhaps social media outlets such as Twitter or LinkedIn.

MAPPING RESOURCES WITHIN AND BEYOND THE SCHOOL GATES

The image that follows is some ideas on how you might begin to map your resources within the school and wider community. You can utilise an incomplete version of this to be able to explore as a wider staff team. As it will be particular to your own setting, you can also include the names of organisations or any resources to support SEND. With this, you can start to have a sense of what is available within your own setting, or perhaps what you think might enhance what you already have.

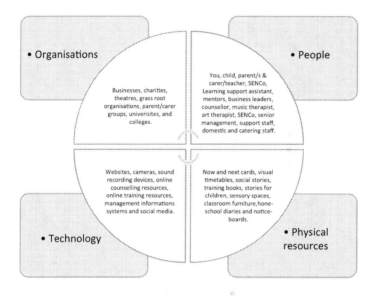

Organisations

Businesses, charities, theatres, grass root organisations, parent/carer groups, univerisites, and colleges.

People

You, child, parent/s & carer/teacher, SENCo, Learning support assistant, mentors, business leaders, counsellor, music therapist, art therapist, SENCo, senior management, support staff, domestic and catering staff.

Technology

Websites, cameras, sound recording devices, online counselling resources, online training resources, management informations systems and social media.

Physical resources

Now and next cards, visual timetables, social stories, training books, stories for children, sensory spaces, classroom furniture, hone-school diaries and notice-boards.

None of the tools offered under each section can work in isolation. The phrase "it takes a village to raise a child" is an important one; it asserts the need for a community to draw together to support a child. Interventions and support within school are important to ensure that a child belongs and is supported. But without drawing upon the assets and resources of those around the child and the wider school community, then it will be harder to fully support a child and their family when things are difficult.

BIBLIOGRAPHY

American Psychiatric Association. (1968). *Diagnostic and Statistical Manual of Mental Disorders* (2nd ed.). Washington: American Psychiatric Publishing.

American Psychiatric Association. (2013). *Diagnostic and Statistical Manual of Mental Disorders* (5th ed.). Washington: American Psychiatric Publishing.

Beat Eating Disorders. (2023, January 19). *Get Information and Support.* Retrieved from Beat Eating Disorders: https://www.beateatingdisorders.org.uk/get-information-and-support/support-someone-else/worried-about-a-pupil/

Beumont, P. (1971). Small handwriting in some patients with anorexia nervosa. *The British Journal of Psychiatry*, 349-351.

Broadwin, I. T. (1932). A contribution to the study of truancy. *Orthopsychiatry*, 2(3), 253-259.

Brooks, R. (2019). *The Trauma and Attachment-Aware Classroom: A Practical Guide to Supporting Children Who Have Encountered Trauma and Adverse Childhood Experiences.* London, UK: Jessica Kingsley.

Burton, V., & Revell, L. (2017). Professional curiosity in child protection: Thinking the unthinkable in a neo-liberal world. *The British Journal of Social Work*, 48(6), 1508-1523. https://doi.org/10.1093/bjsw/bcx123

Casey, Louise (2015). *Reflections on Child Sexual Exploitation.* London: Departments for Communities and Local Government.

Centers for Disease Control and Prevention. (2022, January 18). *The Public Health Approach to Violence Reduction.* Retrieved January 4, 2023, from Violence Prevention: https://www.cdc.gov/violenceprevention/about/publichealthapproach.html

Clements, L., & Aiello, L. A. (2001). Institutionalising parent carer blame. Available at https://cerebra.org.uk/wp-content/

uploads/2021/07/Final-Parent-Blame-Report-20-July-21-02. pdf last accessed 14.06.2023

Clements, L., & George, K. (2023). 'Warrior Mothers and Fathers', in *Square Pegs: Inclusivity, Compassion and Fitting In – a Guide for Schools* by Fran Morgan, Ellie Costello. Carmarthen: Crown House Publishing Ltd.

Creswell, C., Waite, P., & Cooper, P. J. (2014). Assessment and management of anxiety disorders in children and adolescents. *Archives of Disease in Childhood, 99,* 674–678.

Crudgington, H., & Ougrin, D. (2022, March). NICE guidelines for self-harm: A new school of thought (A. F. Health, Ed.). *The Bridge.* https://doi.org/10.13056/acamh.19618

Department for Education. (2017). Child sexual exploitation definition and guide for practitioners. Retrieved January 9, 2023, from https://www.gov.uk/government/publications/child -sexual-exploitation-definition-and-guide-for-practitioners

Dickens, J., Taylor, J., Cook, L., Cossar, J., Garstang, J., Hallett, N., Molloy, E., Rennolds, N., Rimmer, J., Sorensen, P., & Wate, R. (2022, December). Learning for the future: final analysis of serious case reviews, 2017 to 2019. London. UK: Published by Department for Education. Available from https://assets. publishing.service.gov.uk/government/uploads/system/ uploads/attachment_data/file/1123286/Learning_for_the_ future_-_final_analysis_of_serious_case_reviews__2017_ to_2019.pdf

Edwards, D. J. (2021, March 16). *Are School-Based Interventions for Depression and Anxiety Symptoms Effective?* Retrieved from https://www.acamh.org/research-digest/are-school-based-interventions-for-depression-and-anxiety-symptoms-effective/

El-Khodari, B., & Samara, M. (2020). Effectiveness of a school-based intervention on the students' mental health after exposure to war-related trauma. *Front Psychiatry.* https://doi. org/10.3389/fpsyt.2019.01031

Evans, S. W., Schultz, B. K., DeMars, C. E., & Davis, H. (2011). Effectiveness of the challenging horizons after-school program for young adolescents with ADHD. *Behavior Therapy.* https://doi.org/10.1016/j.beth.2010.11.008

Gale, C. G., & Millichamp, J. (2016). Generalised anxiety disorder in children and adolescents. *BMJ Clinical Evidence, 13.*

Gee, B., Reynolds, S., Carroll, S., Orchard, B., Clarke, F., Martin, T., & Wilson, D. (2020). Practitioner review: Effectiveness of indicated school-based interventions for adolescent depression and anxiety – A meta-analytic review. *Journal of Child Psychology and Psychiatry, 61*, 739–756.

Gov.uk. (2022a, July 5). Pupil absence in schools in England autumn term 2021/22. Retrieved from Explore Education Statistics: https://explore-education-statistics.service.gov.uk/find-statistics/pupil-absence-in-schools-in-england-autumn-term

Gov.uk. (2022b, November 19). School discipline and exclusions. Retrieved from https://www.gov.uk/school-discipline-exclusions/exclusions

Gov.uk. (2023, February 4). '06 – Absence rates by pupil characteristic' from 'Pupil absence in schools in England'. Retrieved from Explore Education Statistics: https://explore-education-statistics.service.gov.uk/data-tables/permalink/82b4f664-2119-4333-2dc2-08dafaf734a0

Hackett, S. (2014). *Children and Young People with Harmful Sexual Behaviour.* Devon: Research in Practice. Retrieved January 11, 2023, from https://tce.researchinpractice.org.uk/wp-content/uploads/2020/05/children_and_young_people_with_harmful_sexual_behaviours_research_review_2014.pdf

Hartmann, T. (2015). *ADHD and the Edison Gene: A Drug-Free Approach to Managing the Unique Qualities of Your Child.* Rochester, Vermont: Park Street Press.

Hickle, K., & Hallett, S. (2016). Mitigating harm: Considering harm reduction principles with sexually exploited young people. *Children and Society, 30*(4), 302–313.

Hollis, V., & Belton, E. (2017). *Children and Young People Who Engage in Technology-Assisted Harmful Sexual Behaviour.* NSPCC. Retrieved January 11, 2023, from https://learning.nspcc.org.uk/media/1083/exploring-technology-assisted-harmful-sexual-behaviour.pdf

Honos-Webb, L. (2010). *The Gift of ADHD: How to Transform Your Child's Problems into Strengths.* Oakland, California: New Harbinger.

House of Commons. (2006). *Education and Skills – Third Report.* Retrieved June 21, 2023, from https://publications.parliament.uk/pa/cm200506/cmselect/cmeduski/478/47805.htm#:~:text=Brief%20history%20of%20Special

%20Educational%20Needs%20(SEN)&text=Many%20chi
ldren%20were%20considered%20to,educational%20treat
ment%22%20in%20separate%20schools

International Classification of Diseases. (n.d.). *ICD-10 Version 2019*. Retrieved from Eating Disorders: https://icd.who.int/browse10/2019/en#/F50

Leeds Safeguarding Children Partnership. (2021). *Professional Curiosity*. Retrieved January 12, 2023, from Leeds Safeguarding Children Partnership: https://www.leedsscp.org.uk/practitioners/improving-practice/professional-curiosity

Lefevere, M., Hickle, K., & Lurcock, B. (2017, December). Building trust with children and young people at risk of children exploitation: The professional challenges. *The British Journal of Social Work, 47*(8), 2456–2473.

Leninger, M., Dyches, T., Prater, M., & Heath, M. (2010, March). Teaching students with obsessive compulsive disorder. *Intervention in School and Clinic, 45*(4), 221–231.

Manchester Safeguarding Partnership. (2023). Professional curiosity resources practitioners. Retrieved from https://www.manchestersafeguardingpartnership.co.uk/resource/professional-curiosity-resources-practitioners/

Mason-Jones, A., & Loggie, J. (2020, March). Child sexual exploitation. An analysis of serious case reviews in England: Poor communication, incorrect assumptions and adolescent neglect. *Journal of Public Health, 28*, 62–68.

May, H., Kloess, J. A., & Hamilton-Giachritis, C. E. (2021). Young people's experience of attending a theater-in-education program on Criminal Sexual Exploitation. *Frontiers in Psychology, 12*.

Mental Health First Aid International. (2020, April). What are eating disorders. Retrieved from https://mhfa.com.au/sites/default/files/MHFA_eatdis_guidelines_A4_2013.pdf

Mentally Healthy Schools. (n.d.). *Child Criminal Exploitation*. Retrieved January 12, 2023, from Mentally Healthy Schools: https://mentallyhealthyschools.org.uk/risks-and-protective-factors/vulnerable-children/child-criminal-exploitation/

Murali, K., Jon, A., & Palmer, R. L. (2010). Micrographia and hypophonia in anorexia nervosa. *International Journal of Eating Disorders, 12*, 762–765.

NHS. (2019, March 14). *Overview – Bipolar Disorder*. Retrieved from NHS: https://www.nhs.uk/mental-health/conditions

/bipolar-disorder/overview/#:~:text=Bipolar%20disorder
%20can%20occur%20at,likely%20to%20develop
%20bipolar%20disorder

National Institute for Health and Care Excellence. (2022, September 7). Self harm: Assessment, management and preventing recurrence. Retrieved December 21, 2022, from https://www.nice.org.uk/guidance/ng225/resources/ selfharm-assessment-management-and-preventing- recurrence-pdf-66143837346757

National Institute of Mental Health. (2022, May 30). *What is Psychosis*. Retrieved from National Institute of Mental Health: https://www.nimh.nih.gov/health/topics/schizophrenia/ raise/what-is-psychosis

NHS. (2021, December 24). *Attention Deficit Hyperactivity Disorder*. Retrieved from https://www.nhs.uk/conditions /attention-deficit-hyperactivity-disorder-adhd/ diagnosis/#:~:text=To%20be%20diagnosed%20with %20ADHD,symptoms%20of%20hyperactivity%20and %20impulsiveness.&text=To%20be%20diagnosed%20wit h%20ADHD%2C%20your%20child%20must%20also%20

No Isolation. (2021). *Socially Excluded: Over Half a Million Children Suffer from Prolonged Absence from School*. London: No Isolation. Retrieved December 20, 2022, from https://d1h06bsnqv2xsg.cloudfront.net/Pdf/HalfAMillionChi ldrenMissOutOnSchool_Report_NoIsolation_Sep2021F.pdf

Papyrus. (n.d.). Building suicide-safer schools and colleges: A guide for teachers and staff. Cheshire, United Kingdom. Retrieved from https://www.papyrus-uk.org/schools-guide/

Papyrus. (n.d.). *Self Harm*. Retrieved December 21, 2022, from Papyrus: https://www.papyrus-uk.org/wp-content/uploads /2020/01/001159-PAPYRUS-Leaflet_Self-Harm.pdf

Piacentini, J., Bergman, R., Keller, M., & McCracken, J. (2013). Functional impairment in children and adolescents with obsessive-compulsive disorder, *Journal of Child and Adolescent Psychopharmacology, 13*(Suppl 1), S61–S69. https://doi.org/10.1089/104454603322126359

Pontin, E., Peters, S., Lobban, F., Rogers, A., & Morriss, R. K. (2009). Enhanced relapse prevention for bipolar disorder: A qualitative investigation of value perceived for service users and care coordinators. *Implementation Science, 4*(4), https://doi.org/10.1186/1748-5908-4-4.

Siegel, D. (1999). *The Developing Mind: How Relationships and the Brain Interact to Shape Who We Are.* New York: Guilford Press.

Stern, K. (2022). *The Excludables: From Mainstream to Prison Education.* Woodbridge: John Catt Educational Ltd.

Stone, N. (2018). Child criminal exploitation: 'County lines', trafficking and cuckooing. *Youth Justice, 18*, 185–293.

Striegel-Moore, R. H., Rosselli, F., Perrin, N., DeBar, L., Wilson, G. T., May, A., & Kraemer, H. C. (2009). Gender difference in the prevalence of eating disorder symptoms. *The International Journal of Eating Disorders, 42*(5), 471–474. https://doi.org/10.1002/eat.20625

Tenconi, E., Collantoni, E., Meregalli, V., Bonello, E., Zanetti, T., Veronese, A., & Meneguzzo, P. (2021, April 20). Clinical and cognitive functioning changes after partial hospitalization in patients with Anorexia Nervosa. *Frontiers in Psychiatry.* https://doi.org/10.3389/fpsyt.2021.653506

The Association of Directors of Children's Services Ltd. (2018). *ADCS Leading Children's Services.* Retrieved January 23, 2023, from Contextual Safeguarding: https://adcs.org.uk/assets/documentation/Contextual_Safeguarding_briefing_FINAL.pdf

The Children's Society. (2018, March 2). *Children and Young People Trafficked for the Purpose of Criminal Exploitation in Relation to County Lines: A Toolkit for Professionals.* Retrieved June 30, 2022, from The Children's Society: https://www.childrenssociety.org.uk/sites/default/files/2021-01/exploitation-toolkit.pdf

The Children's Society. (2021, April 27). *Defining Criminal Exploitation.* Retrieved June 30, 2022, from The Children's Society: https://www.childrenssociety.org.uk/information/professionals/resources/defining-child-criminal-exploitation

The Office for National Statistics. (2022). *Young People's Substance Misuse Treatment Statistics 2020 to 2021: Report.* Office for Health Improvement and Disparities. Retrieved January 24, 2023, from https://www.gov.uk/government/statistics/substance-misuse-treatment-for-young-people-statistics-2020-to-2021/young-peoples-substance-misuse-treatment-statistics-2020-to-2021-report

Thompson, I., Tawell, A., & Daniels, H. (2021). Conflicts in professional concern and the exclusion of pupils with SEMH in England. *Emotional and Behavioural Difficulties, 26,* 31–45.

Timpson, E. (2019). *The Timpson Review of School Exclusions.* London: Crown Copyright. Retrieved November 19, 2022, from https://assets.publishing.service.gov.uk/government /uploads/system/uploads/attachment_data/file/807862/ Timpson_review.pdf

Turn the Page. (2023, January 11). Retrieved from Lucy Faithfull Foundation: https://ecsa.lucyfaithfull.org/turn-page

UNICEF. (n.d.). A Summary of the UN Convention on the Rights of the Child. Retrieved May 30, 2022, from https://www.unicef. org.uk/rights-respecting-schools/wp-content/uploads/sites /4/2017/01/Summary-of-the-UNCRC.pdf

University of Bedfordshire. (2023, February 5). Safer Young Lives. Retrieved from Safer Young Lives Research Centre: https://www.beds.ac.uk/sylrc/

Warnock, M. (1978). *Report of the Committee of Enquiry into the Education of Children and Young People.* London: Her Majesty's Stationery Office.

Watson, L., & Lask, B. (n.d.). *A Short Introduction to Understanding and Supporting Children with Eating Disorders.* Jessica Kinglsey Publishers.

Wells, J. (2006). *Touch and Go Joe – An Adolescent's Experience of OCD.* London: Jessica Kingsley.

Winston's Wish. (2019, June). *Guide to Supporting Grieving Children in Education.* Retrieved from Winston's Wish: https://www.winstonswish.org/wp-content/uploads/2019 /06/Guide-to-supporting-grieving-children-in-education.pdf

Zandt, D., & Barrett, D. (2021). *Creative Ways to Help Children Manage Anxiety.* London: Jessica Kingsley Publishers.

INDEX

Printed in the United States
by Baker & Taylor Publisher Services